THE AWAKENING GIANT

THE AWAKENING GIANT

THE MIRACULOUS STORY OF THE
Full Gospel Business Men's Fellowship International

Val Fotherby

Marshall Pickering
An Imprint of HarperCollins*Publishers*

Marshall Pickering is an Imprint of
HarperCollins*Religious*
Part of HarperCollins*Publishers*
77–85 Fulham Palace Road, London W6 8JB
www.christian-publishing.co.uk

First published in Great Britain
in 2000 by Marshall Pickering

1 3 5 7 9 10 8 6 4 2

A catalogue record for this book
is available from the British Library.

ISBN 0 551 03234 0

Printed and bound in Great Britain by
Caledonian International Book Manufacturing Ltd, Glasgow

Contents

Foreword

Have you ever asked yourself ... what would the apostles and disciples do if they arrived in the world today?

Val Fotherby has answered this question in *The Awakening Giant*. The inspiring stories of individual men transformed by faith in Jesus Christ makes this an extraordinary book. The power of inspiration in the lives of men and women has always been a fascinating subject. Val and her husband, David, have been long time friends of our family and as a Director of the FGBMFI, David has participated in many of the greatest events in Christianity since the first century.

I know you will enjoy reading *The Awakening Giant* as much as I have.

Richard Shakarian
International President
Full Gospel Business Men's Fellowship International

Acknowledgements

It has been a great privilege to write this book, and I am grateful for the support, encouragement and help of so many people. First and foremost, my husband David, whose idea the book was and who has criticized, suggested different points of view and, above all, encouraged me throughout. International President Richard Shakarian and his wife Vangie; John Carrette, the Executive Vice President whose enthusiasm has been uplifting; Ron Weinbender and the office staff at Irvine; and, last but not least, all those people who were prepared to give up their time for interviews, telephone calls, e-mails, faxes and letters. A very big 'thank you' to everyone.

For those countries which have not been included, please accept my apologies. This book was not intended to be in any way a definitive history of the Fellowship, but was meant to give the reader an understanding of the growth and work of the FGBMFI worldwide. Above all, it has been my intention to show how God can take ordinary men and women, fill them with His Holy Spirit, and enabling them to become part of His army of laymen, the Awakening Giant.

Preface

The Full Gospel Business Men's Fellowship International was born out of prophecy. As far back as the nineteenth century, God had set in motion a series of events that would eventually result in the Shakarian family leaving Armenia and moving to Los Angeles. From this family emerged one of the greatest Christian men of the twentieth century, Demos Shakarian.

More than fifty years ago, Dr Charles Price, a close friend of Demos, had prophesied to him regarding the great army of laymen that God would raise up in the last days to bring in the final harvest of His Kingdom. In the 1950s, Dr Mordecai Hamm, the great Southern preacher and evangelist who introduced Billy Graham to Christ, sought out Demos at a hotel in Houston and prophesied almost identical words to those of Dr Price. 'Full Gospel Business Men's Fellowship International is God's instrument to awaken laymen – the sleeping giant of evangelism.'

Around the same time, God gave evangelist Tommy Hicks a most powerful prophecy on this same theme, which is detailed in Appendix A.

All of these prophetic words dovetailed with the vision given by God to Demos for the Full Gospel Business Men's Fellowship International, so that the concept of the Fellowship being part of that awakening giant has remained a powerful image throughout its history.

In September 1999, Pastor Rick Gillis from Texas gave a prophetic word at the UK and Ireland national convention in Blackpool. In that prophecy, God spoke of the Fellowship being like Gulliver, appearing as a giant to the people and having the ropes cut to release it from the things that were holding it back. He said that the Fellowship, like Gulliver, was now free to travel, and that it would take the Gospel to the nations of the world with a new fire and a new anointing of the Holy Spirit.

Introduction

Clifton's Cafeteria, downtown Los Angeles, Saturday morning. Outside, young men were handing out *Voice* magazines. A breakfast of the Full Gospel Business Men's Fellowship International was advertised. At any moment, you might have expected Demos Shakarian, and perhaps Oral Roberts or Miner Arganbright, to walk in through the doorway, pick up their breakfast on the ground floor and climb the stairs to the upper room. Except that this was nearly fifty years on, and the *Voice* magazines and all the signs were in Spanish.

David, my husband, and I were privileged to be the only non-Latin people at this outreach breakfast. One of the young men from Guatemala, Luis Aquindo Fernandez, over for the FGBMFI world convention, felt that God had told him to reach out to the families and friends of the people from Central America living in the Los Angeles area, to hear men from their home countries tell how Jesus had changed their lives. About a hundred people were there, mainly men, and of those, many were young. There was a great sense of excitement and expectancy, as well as a sense of history, as some members of the Fellowship stood to give short testimonies just as they had throughout the years since the 1950s.

Men shared about how God had healed their families. For one it was his son, healed of cancer; another whose son, seriously injured by a camera falling on him on a TV production set, was now healed and videoing the meeting that morning; another whose daughter had been healed of anorexia; and one healed of serious mental illness. One member had his financial needs met to attend a world convention, and a former financial assistant to two FGBMFI presidents told how God has blessed his business to the extent that he is now able to travel around Guatemala, training men in the chapters. The former head of the Guatemalan air force shared how God has enabled him to run a small airline that gives away seats to people going to minister in chapters. Colonel Armando Cifuentes, now President of FGBMFI in Colombia told how, as a fitness fanatic, he had met Roberto Velasquez, hosting the meeting that morning, and was taken to an FGBMFI meeting. Having turned his life over to Jesus, he had gone back to Colombia to start the work there. He is now President of FGBMFI in Colombia.

Luis Aquindo Fernandez talked about how important it is that the Fellowship encourages men back into their churches. Luis said it is good because it brings the wife, children and wider family back together again. FGBMFI is also important, he said, because it teaches how to give and tithe to the Church.

At one point in the meeting, people were asked to write out their petitions and put them in the 'miracle' box. John Carrette lifted up that box of prayers, saying that Jesus had destroyed the power of Satan and that he believed the petitions would become performed miracles. When he asked if anyone wanted to ask Jesus into their lives, to change them and set them on a new path, around twenty men responded.

There was a freshness about the testimonies that morning, a sense of reality that made Jesus alive in the room. As John Carrette stood to draw the breakfast meeting to a close, he reminded the people about the men who had been in that room nearly fifty years before. 'You,' he said, 'have the same Jesus Christ in you as they had, the same Holy Spirit as they had. Hear well, because you have the same mission that these men had. That vision that came into being in this room has given birth to around 6,000 chapters, and tens of millions of people around the world have come to Jesus. God has placed that same vision within you. The anointing is on the vision. You men who have the vision, the same things can happen in your chapters – you could give birth to thousands of chapters, and give birth to people coming to know Jesus. Go out from this place and take this layman's ministry around the nations.'

ONE

Almost Over Before It Began

Eighteen men waited in Clifton's Cafeteria for the arrival of Demos Shakarian. It was to be the first meeting of the Full Gospel Business Men's Fellowship. Over the previous sixteen days, Demos had organized a series of meetings for Oral Roberts – the biggest he had ever been involved with; more than 200,000 people had attended. At the final meeting, Demos had announced this Saturday morning breakfast to the crowd of 12,500 who had come to hear Oral Roberts. He had also contacted as many Christian business men as he could. This morning, Demos could scarcely contain his excitement as he drove to downtown Los Angeles. Surely there would be a big crowd – after all, he'd given God a size-able helping hand with his efforts. His face dropped as he walked through the door and saw the size of the group waiting. Eighteen men! Oral Roberts had come along as the speaker, and after talking to the men for about twenty minutes he began to pray. 'Lord, Jesus, let this Fellowship grow in Your strength alone. Send it marching in Your power across the nation, across the world. We give You thanks right now, Lord Jesus, that we see a little group of people in a cafeteria, but You see a thousand chapters.' Those words sparked life into the group of men: they all joined hands and marched around the room singing 'Onward Christian Soldiers'.

The Shakarian family had come to the USA from Armenia early in the twentieth century. In Los Angeles, the family had prospered, financially – they owned the largest dairy herd in the United States – and spiritually. Demos, in particular, became well known in both the business and Christian communities. One of the many remarkable things about this man was the way in which he understood the role God had prepared for him: that of a helper, someone who was to enable others to reach their potential.

Throughout the 1940s, Demos had been involved, at first in a small way but eventually on a very large scale, in organizing meetings for leading evangelists of the day. Billy Graham and Oral Roberts are perhaps the two best known of those who owed a great deal to the organization and support of the Shakarians. Along with Dr Charles Price and Tommy Hicks, Roberts was highly influential in encouraging Demos in the start of a new movement in 1951. Demos had long been concerned at the lack of men in churches and Christian meetings, and he felt compelled to provide an opportunity to bring men together in places that were familiar to them, hotels and restaurants, to hear the stories of those whose lives had been changed by the power of Jesus. He had seen tremendous success through the many different meetings he had organized, but now he felt that God was leading him in a new direction.

Business men's groups, such as the Rotary, the Lions and Kiwanis Clubs, had shown Demos the benefits of being able to meet in a relaxed atmosphere, discuss what was happening and hear business colleagues talking about their lives. What he wanted to do was to add a spiritual dimension to the social fellowship, and with his experience of organizing Christian meetings for nearly twenty years Demos felt this was what God was calling him to do.

Dr Charles Price was an Englishman who trained as a lawyer at Oxford University. Following a conversion experience in America, he had settled there and became one of the greatest teachers of the early Pentecostal movement. He had prayed for the sister of Demos when she had been seriously injured in a car accident; her pelvis was crushed and she had serious burns over her back, and the doctors gave little hope of recovery. As Dr Price laid hands on the girl, her body shook for twenty minutes, but during that experience God healed her. This not only convinced Demos of God's power to heal, but was also the start of a close friendship between the two men. They would meet regularly over a meal and mull over what was happening on the Christian scene. On one of these occasions, Dr Price leaned across the table, took Demos by the hand and gave him a prophecy relating to a last great revival that would come through 'laymen', ordinary men and women who would tell those around them that Jesus was the answer to all their needs.

You're about to witness one of the major events foretold in the Bible. 'And it shall come to pass afterward, that I will pour out My Spirit upon all flesh ...' It will happen in your lifetime, Demos, and you will play a part in it. This revival will not come through professional preachers ... but will happen spontaneously – all over the world to ordinary men and women – people in shops, offices and factories. Laymen will be His most important channel – not the clergy, or the theologians, or the great gifted preachers, but men and women with ordinary jobs in the ordinary world. I won't live long enough to see it, but you will.[1]

These words stirred Demos, but it took a number of years before he was to take the step towards bringing about a laymen's organization to become known as the Full Gospel Business Men's Fellowship International. Many times in the subsequent years, Dr Price talked to Demos about how the laymen were the ones whom God would use to bring in the final harvest. Demos shared on numerous occasions with Oral Roberts, who asked him how it was going to be done, and who was going to prepare and train the laymen to do it. Later, when Demos asked the question of Charles Price, he said, 'Demos, the Holy Spirit can do more in a split second than all the talking in the world.'

During the year following that first meeting at Clifton's Cafeteria, all faith and confidence that this Fellowship was of God gradually drained away. Far from a thousand chapters, there was still only one. Disappointment and frustration set in as Demos travelled widely, trying to promote the Fellowship, spending thousands of dollars of his own money in the process. No contributions came in and no other groups were started. He had even travelled to the Pentecostal World Conference in London with David du Plessis, the first time Demos had left America, but his ideas fell on deaf ears. It seemed that he had misunderstood what God wanted him to do, and all that was left was to admit this and wind up the Fellowship.

How often it seems to happen that in the darkest of moments, God suddenly shines His light making the way ahead plain to see. Saturday 29 December, Demos had decided, would be the last breakfast of the Fellowship, and on the Friday evening prior to this, he shared his disappointments with the evangelist Tommy Hicks, a very good friend who was staying with Demos and Rose. Tommy understood what Demos was going through, and when he went upstairs that night, instead of getting into bed, he got down on his face before God in prayer.

Demos was exhausted from the tears he had shed during the past week in the belief that the Fellowship had come to an end, but knew that he would not be able to sleep. His friend Miner Arganbright had been telling him he didn't know when to quit, and so had Rose. All that week she had been telling Demos that although everything else he had done had been successful, this was not working. He told Rose to go to bed, but he himself stayed in the lounge, where he too prostrated himself on the floor, weeping and praying in tongues. And into his distress, God spoke. Demos knew this voice. At the age of 13, when he had received the power of the Holy Spirit in a dramatic way and had instantly been healed of deafness, God had spoken and said, 'Demos, will you ever doubt my power?' Since then, he had heard God's voice many times.

At three o'clock that morning, when Rose, also unable to sleep, came to join him, he was still in the same position. Sitting at the organ she began to play quietly, and as the music filled the room Demos saw the ceiling apparently recede to be replaced by a daytime sky. Rose stopped playing and began to speak in tongues; she gave the interpretation: 'My son, I knew you before you were born. I have guided you every step of the way. Now I am going to show you the purpose of your life.'

As he listened to her words, Demos felt as if he was leaving his body, although he remained on his knees. It was as if he rose higher and higher above the earth until he could see the whole of the United States, from the west to the east. What he saw terrified him. Millions of men standing shoulder to shoulder, yet separate, lifeless, their eyes staring straight ahead, unblinking and unseeing. But the vision did not stop there. As the earth seemingly turned slowly, he saw the different continents of South America, Africa and Asia. Just as a camera can zoom in at a football game to show first the stadium, then the players, then the detail on the football, his vision seemed to move in on these millions of men. He was able to see tiny details of thousands and thousands of faces. Yet again he saw startling close-ups of brown, black and white faces, each one wretched and lifeless. He cried out, 'Lord, what's the matter with them! Lord, help them!'

Completely unaware of the vision that Demos was receiving, Rose began to prophesy again: 'My son, what you see next is going to happen very soon.'

Demos saw the earth revolve again, but this time the scene was so different. No longer was it one of death, but of life. Faces were transformed; the eyes of the men shone with joy – they were glowing. Heads were lifted up and hands were raised towards heaven; they had been brought out of a prison of isolation to be joined together by love. Death had turned to life.

As the vision faded, Demos got up, somewhat stiffly, from his knees. It was half past three in the morning. As he shared what he had seen with Rose, they both knew that the Lord was telling them to go on with the Fellowship and that He would use it to fulfil the vision.

As Demos and Rose passed Tommy's door on their way to bed, he called out to them. Tommy was still fully clothed – he even had his coat on. Lying face downwards on the floor, he had been supporting Demos as best he knew how: in prayer. He wanted to know what had been happening because, as never before, he had experienced the power of God pouring through him and through the house in waves. He told Demos that time and again he had tried to get up off his knees, but every time he stood up the power of the Holy Spirit threw him back on to the floor. It was that same night that he too received a vision of what God was going to do through him in Argentina. (In 1954 Tommy was to speak to over three million people in that country and record 300,000 decisions for Jesus.) There was no sleep for any of them after such an outpouring.

The week prior to receiving this great vision from God, Demos had gone to the Saturday morning breakfast at Clifton's Cafeteria. At the door he had been met by his friend, business man Miner Arganbright. 'You don't know when you're whipped. I wouldn't give you five cents for this outfit,' he said to Demos. Now, one week later, walking into Clifton's, Demos was met by the same man. This time Miner handed him an envelope. Demos fully expected it to be Miner's resignation, given that he had already written off the Fellowship. However, when he opened the envelope he could scarcely believe his eyes – there was a cheque made out to the Full Gospel Business Men's Fellowship International for one thousand dollars! 'This work,' said Miner, 'is going to spread around the world.' What a turn-around! Another man, Thomas Nickel, prompted by God, travelled all night to be at the breakfast meeting. He told Demos that the Fellowship needed a 'voice' and, as a printer, that was what he was pre-pared to provide. He would print a magazine of testimonies that would be the voice of the FGBMFI.

TWO

The Holy Spirit – the Spearhead

'We didn't know exactly where we were going, but we knew we were moving with God!'

The Full Gospel Business Men's Fellowship International was birthed by prophecy and God confirmed this to Demos many times. One evening, while Demos was staying in a hotel in Houston, Dr Mordecai Hamm, the great evangelist who introduced Billy Graham to Christ, asked to see him. The two had never previously met or even spoken, but Dr Hamm said that he knew more about the Fellowship than Demos did because God had given him a revelation of the last days. As they talked together, Mordecai prophesied that: 'Full Gospel Business Men's Fellowship International is God's instrument to awaken laymen – the sleeping giant of evangelism.' These were almost identical to the words spoken by Dr Charles Price.

What made this even more remarkable was that Dr Hamm was responsible for training over 10,000 preachers in the United States at that time. 'I have been praying for many years,' he said to Demos, 'but a few days ago God spoke to me and said that this Fellowship is the instrument He is going to use in the last days. This is the moment, son. Don't ever look back.'

Demos shared some years later that it was not until that week in Houston that his eyes were opened: only then did he realize that Dr Charles Price's words about the laymen bringing in the harvest of the last days referred to the FGBMFI. 'It almost scared me,' he said, 'except I knew I was doing what God wanted me to do. He was going to make something out of this and I knew I was in His hands. God reminded me again that He had given me His Son, He had given me His authority and He had given me His Name. There was nothing more He could give me or that I needed.'

A further prophetic confirmation was given through his friend, Tommy Hicks. Tommy had seen a vision of the world: as it came into view, there was lightning and thunder. Suddenly he saw a great giant whose arms stretched from sea to sea while his feet seemed to reach to the North Pole and his head to the South. The giant struggled to get up and throw off all the debris that was holding him down. Then, slowly, this great giant lifted his hands towards the heavens, as though praising the Lord.

The giant in this vision was made up of hundreds of thousands of people from all over the world – Africa, England, Russia, China, America, and so on. These were ordinary men and women whom God had anointed to minister salvation and healing to the people of the whole world. This vision of the awakening giant confirmed to Demos, once again, the things that God wanted to do through the FGBMFI.[1]

Clearly, one 'chapter' (the name given to the group in Los Angeles) did not make an international fellowship, but following that extraordinary experience in December 1952, Demos no longer doubted God's plan for the FGBMFI. It was Tommy Hicks, not Demos, who opened the second chapter, following a crusade held in Sioux Falls, South Dakota. When it came to the end of the final meeting, he asked if any men present were interested in forming a local FGBMFI chapter. 'It looked like the whole room came forward,' he said later, when telephoning the good news to

Demos that the second chapter had been born. Tommy rigged up a loudspeaker system so that Demos was able to speak over the phone to all the men gathered in the room.

Many of the early chapters that followed came about as a result of crusades held by the three leading healing evangelists of the 1950s: Tommy Hicks, Oral Roberts and William Branham. 'In a sense, FGBMFI was one of the most important and lasting institutions fostered by the healing movement of the 1950s. Not only did the Fellowship open up new opportunities for the healing evangelists, it became at one and the same time the "product" and "platform" for the healing revival.'[2]

The growth from that tentative beginning became nothing short of explosive. Not only did the Fellowship grow through the help of these evangelists, but also *Voice* magazine began to have an enormous impact. As well as telling the stories of men whose lives had been turned around by Jesus, this magazine also contained 'Six Steps To Salvation', outlining how people could become Christians. *Voice*, as well as the radio programme *Breakfast-Broadcast* which went out every Saturday morning from Clifton's Cafeteria on radio station KRKD from 8.30 to 9.30, helped to open more chapters and bring in subscriptions from all parts of America and abroad. Christian business men had discovered a way of reaching men for God that was to change their own lives and those of the men, and women, they invited to outreach breakfasts, luncheons or dinners.

Tommy Ashcraft typifies the kind of man for whom the FGBMFI was life-changing. He ran a very large successful bakery business in Atlanta, Georgia. One day he received a phone call from Houston. A friend at the other end said, 'Tommy, I've found something which I think will really interest you. I know what you want to do, and this will be right down your alley.' He went on to tell how he had met Demos

Shakarian and about the organization to bring business men to Jesus. 'Demos is forming chapters of what he calls the Full Gospel Business Men's Fellowship International, and we want you to help us get a chapter started in Atlanta.'[3]

This was what Tommy wanted to hear. He had been brought up in a Christian home, was married at a young age and had built up a successful business. However, he had become heavily involved in gambling, drinking and womanizing; this had almost wrecked his marriage, but then his wife became a Christian. Through her prayers and those of her church, Tommy eventually came to know Jesus for himself. For some time, looking back over his life, he wondered where the business men were who could have helped him. Surely there were men of God around in the business world, but where had they been when he needed them? This telephone call was to change all that.

Tommy got a small group of men together and they organized a breakfast meeting for a Saturday morning. He invited business colleagues, presidents of flour mills and insurance companies, doctors, lawyers, store managers or owners and even a sprinkling of judges and politicians. Sixty-seven men in all came that morning, and later every one of them signed up to become a member of the FGBMFI. The Atlanta chapter became one of the largest in the Fellowship, regularly getting 1,600 men at breakfast meetings.

It was the practice for every member to bring a guest to each breakfast. One morning, the friend Tommy had arranged to bring couldn't come at the last moment, and Tommy felt uncomfortable with a vacant chair next to him. An inner voice told him to get up and find someone to take the place of his guest. He walked into the lobby, but it was empty, and when he looked outside it was raining. After standing for several minutes, Tommy heard the voice again, telling him to go out on to the pavement. Rather reluctantly, because of the rain, he stepped outside. The only person in sight was a man sitting with his back against the building. The voice said, 'There's your guest.'

The man's head was down and his face was difficult to see because of his long, unkempt hair. He was wearing an old brown shirt which didn't look clean, and his ragged trousers were water-soaked up to his knees. To cap it all, an empty wine bottle in a paper bag was lying at his side. Tommy's response was, 'Oh, Lord, not him?' God said, 'Yes, Tommy, he's your guest.'

As Tommy went over and asked if he would be his guest for breakfast in the hotel, the man's face registered surprise. His eyes were bleary and registered little understanding of what was happening, and he had at least three days' growth of beard on his face. Nevertheless, Tommy helped him to his feet and tried to get him through the revolving door – with some difficulty! Eventually the two of them staggered into the dining-room and Tommy more or less pushed him to the seat next to his at the top table. Describing the event, Tommy said, 'The eyes of everyone in the room had followed our wobbling progress with ill-concealed amusement. I know many of them wondered what I was up to.'[4]

By the time Tommy had got the man seated, the start of the breakfast meeting was overdue and there was no time to find out his name or anything about him, but at the back of Tommy's mind the words of Jesus were coming to him, 'Verily I say unto you, inasmuch as you have done it unto one of the least of these my brethren, you have done it unto me.' Tommy stood up and started the meeting. Meanwhile his guest tried to eat the bacon and eggs; he fed his chin and nose more than his mouth, but eventually he got them down.

When the speaker had finished giving his testimony of how Jesus had changed his life, he gave the invitation, always given at FGBMFI meetings, to anyone who wanted to turn their lives over to Jesus. Tommy's guest was the first man to raise his hand, and one of the other men on the table came and knelt beside his chair and 'prayed him through to Jesus'. Everyone in the room witnessed a miracle as this man claimed his salvation and stood on his feet, completely sober. He didn't even look the same as before; he was a new man.

After the meeting was over, Tommy took the opportunity to talk to his guest and heard an amazing story. Two years previously, he had been a respected business man in Atlanta, but he had started drinking and his wife had left him. She took half his business in the divorce settlement, and in remorse he'd drunk the other half. As the result of all this, he'd ended up on skid row, unable to hold down a job. Now he looked Tommy in the eye and said, 'All that's behind me.' Over a relatively short time, this man regained everything he had lost. His wife came back to him and he got his business back; then he, too, started taking men to chapter meetings.

It would be misleading to imply that everything was easy in those early days. In later years, when training men in running chapters, Tommy shared some of the secrets of success. Fasting was a key factor, particularly in the week preceding the breakfast. He also told of how people would travel 250 to 300 miles to be at the breakfast when there were only a few chapters. The Ashcraft family home had four bedrooms and a basement. Friday evenings before the breakfast would see them making up beds for themselves in the basement, with the bedrooms, every sofa and often sleeping bags all over the floors filled with people who wanted to ensure they were part of this wonderful thing that God was doing.

It is little wonder that with men of commitment such as Tommy Ashcraft and many others, the Fellowship grew apace in those early years. The momentum increased as new chapters were added, and from 1953 an annual international convention was held in some large city in the United States.

People were attracted to these meetings by the wonderful testimonies, the singing and the many healings that took place. Without doubt, it was a new move of the Holy Spirit. It was at one of these early conventions that David du Plessis stated that the course of his life and ministry had been changed through the experience of being there. Not only did many of the great 'ministries' give tremendous support to Demos and the FGBMFI, but new men and ministries emerged as a result of the opportunities given to speak and develop in Fellowship meetings and conventions. Laymen were in the forefront of ministry in a new, dynamic way, and it was their testimonies, rather than preaching, that was so effective in reaching men and women with the Gospel. In conventions and weekends for members and friends, preaching and teaching happened, but essentially it was the testimony of business men that was so powerful. (The term 'business men' in this context means anyone from the chairman of the board downward.)

Another important factor in the growth of the Fellowship was Demos himself. Everyone who met him loved him. Tommy Ashcraft says of Demos that he had enough love for a nation. Oral Roberts described him as 'The righteous man who flourished like the palm tree' (Psalm 92:12). He had incredible humility and never pushed himself, always being willing to give place to others. One of the many stories about Demos concerns an event at the World Pentecostal Conference in Jerusalem. Standing in the lobby one evening, Demos saw a man almost doubled over with arthritis, his upper body being parallel with the floor. As he was not a registered delegate, this man was unable to get entry to the auditorium, and the lady with him explained to Demos that he had come for healing. Feeling compassion for the man, Demos loaned him his registration badge but also said he would pray for healing. Immediately Demos prayed that the Lord would touch him, this man stood up straight, completely healed. The whole conference heard the excited shouts of the man and the lady who had brought him.

Within two to three years of the launch of the Fellowship, it became truly 'international'. The Fellowship was less dependent on outside ministries to support it (although they have continued to play an important role), but it was able to send its own men throughout the United States and beyond with the Gospel of Jesus Christ.

Some years later, during an International Congress on World Evangelism in Lausanne, Switzerland, Dr Kuhn of Ashbury Theological Seminary wrote a paper in which he said:

About two decades ago there began to emerge among the non-Pentecostal bodies, phenomena very similar to those marking the charismatic movement at the beginning of the present century.

This movement, perhaps best embodied in the Full Gospel Business Men's Fellowship International, is popularly known as Neo-Pentecostal. It represents a cutting edge of charismatic fervour in the more staid churches.

... In the so-called Western world (including Western Europe), the Full Gospel Business Men's Fellowship International (commonly known as the FGBMFI), has opened the charismatic ministry to laymen. This movement has, by enlisting the energies and gifts of men well placed in the business world, shattered the earlier stereotype by which Pentecostalism was regarded as a phenomenon largely confined to the economically deprived. The FGBMFI is an aggressive and effective instrument of evangelism to all classes, in the United States and abroad.

The International Director and Administrator in the FGBMFI headquarters at Irvine, Ron Weinbender, summed up the FGBMFI as helping to teach men to minister and understand their destiny. Often when men first join the Fellowship they are unable to speak publicly but, learning through the example of those around them, soon they are able to stand up and minister to people in almost any situation. FGBMFI helps to break down barriers between people and opens up opportunities in countries because the members are business men and as such are accepted. Ordinary men are turned into extraordinary men for God.

THREE

Barnstorming America

It was like a fire spreading. Once the Fellowship had started, the momentum for growth was phenomenal. Demos now had the weekly Saturday morning broadcast from Clifton's Cafeteria, *Voice* magazine was increasing its circulation, and each time Oral Roberts had a crusade he gave Demos the opportunity to stand up and speak about the Full Gospel Business Men's Fellowship and to invite the people to break- fast meetings in their town. Men were catching the vision of what God wanted to do and were working to fulfil it. All of these were important, but the driving force of the Fellowship was the Holy Spirit. If there is anything that comes through the writings and spoken words of Demos, it is his consum- mate belief and confidence in the power and the ability of the Holy Spirit as the third person of the Trinity. That is some- thing he has passed to his son, Richard, and which continues to be at the forefront of the Fellowship.

Demos and the men around him started to travel through- out the whole of the United States, sharing the vision that God had given for the Fellowship. Often, when they had gathered a group of men together, one or another would say that God had shown them to do this weeks, months or even years ago. Now they were being provided with the means to go forward. Chapters were started at an incredible rate as men were excited through hearing the remarkable things God was doing in changing lives, healing and baptizing in the Holy Spirit.

In the *Dictionary of Pentecostal and Charismatic Movements*, one writer describes what God had given to Demos.

> The original vision of the FGBMFI was of a non-sectarian fellowship of laity who could come together to share what God had done in their lives without any apology – even if that testimony included healing or tongues or deliverance from demonic forces. The impact of the FGBMFI on the Pentecostal and charismatic movements has been considerable.[1]

The impact of the Fellowship on the Catholic Charismatic Movement began in the latter part of the 1960s when Ray Bullard, FGBMFI chapter president in South Bend, Indiana, opened his home to students and professors from Notre Dame University. After teaching and prayer, several received the baptism in the Holy Spirit. Since that time tens of millions of Catholics around the world have moved in the Charismatic Renewal. In 1974, the Pope gave Demos a special award recognizing the role of FGBMFI in the Catholic Charismatic Movement.

The Seattle chapter was one of the largest groups in the Fellowship. The president, Don Ostrom, was a man who believed God had called him and his wife Marlene to be missionaries in the Philippines. However, a tragic family accident – Marlene's father and sister were killed in a plane crash – forced them to come back to Washington and take over the six nursing homes that her father had owned and operated. Although they fully expected to settle the estate and return to the mission field within a few months, it took three years for the legal matters to be sorted, and by then they felt obligated to stay and run the business. Don was confronted by a painful question: 'How can a man who has been a pastor, an evangelist and a missionary be just a business man?' The Full Gospel Business Men's Fellowship proved to be his answer – and specifically the Seattle chapter. This group soon had over 400 members and saw God move in people's lives. One man was brought to a breakfast following a suicide attempt. In total despair, he had gone into the kitchen of his home and driven a butcher's knife into his chest. Despite profuse bleeding, he survived, and that morning in the Seattle chapter he found the Life-giver, Jesus.

At his first FGBMFI convention in Phoenix, Don learned about giving and receiving. Long concerned as to whether it was right for Christians to have money, he learned that God blesses financially, not so we can have more for ourselves but so that we can use it to bless others. He and his wife eventually came to the place where they were able to give 50 per cent of their income to reach people for Jesus. The Seattle chapter was, and remains to this day, the leader in organizing airlifts to different parts of the world. (Airlifts are when a group of FGBMFI men and women, at their own expense, travel to different countries to share the Gospel.) Consequently, instead of ministering in the Philippines only, Don travelled throughout the USA, Canada and Europe.

The story of another Seattle chapter president, Bob Bignold, is typical of so many members of the FGBMFI. After studying architectural engineering he went into the army and was sent out to Korea after the war there had ended. One day he was waiting for a plane to take him on rest and recreation break; it was coming in to land, bringing others back from their R and R, when it crashed, resulting in the death of all the young men on board. Having just seen his colleagues burned up in their plane, Bob's next air trip was the worst journey of his life, and he developed a fear of death and a concern as to whether there was life afterwards.

When he returned from duties, Bob married, adopted two children and, along with two business partners, set up an architectural business. His father had taught him the importance of setting goals, and he devoted his whole life to developing the business, particularly after having bought out the other partners. Not surprisingly, his wife could not cope with always being second in his life, and she left him. Later he met and married a Christian lady; eventually he too became a Christian, but he was still very business orientated – success to him meant 20 per cent more profit – so when he saw a book around the house called *Power and Praise* he started to read it, thinking it was a motivational book. Through reading this book he was not only healed but received the baptism of the Holy Spirit. Other Christian books followed, many of which mentioned the FGBMFI, and eventually he discovered they had a chapter in Seattle.

An Episcopalian, Bob was used to quiet orderliness in church, but the chapter meeting was nothing like that! The speaker talked about how, as a captain in the Second World War, his shoulder had been blown away and he had been left with one side of his body held together by wires. For thirty years, he had been dependent on drugs until, at one of the FGBMFI dinners, one of the leaders prayed for him and he was healed. In his testimony, he told how when he went to the hospital they could not even find the wires that had held him together! From that day on, Bob has been heavily involved with the Fellowship; he served for seven years as president of the Seattle chapter, becoming an International Director of the Fellowship and travelling abroad on many airlifts, particularly to Japan, where he has gone two or three times a year for ten years – but more of that later.

Another business man who joined in the very early years was Tom Leding. He became International Treasurer of the FGBMFI and worked in the Oklahoma chapters. He had been raised in church, was a great believer of God's word and was determined to be successful in business. Tom knew the importance of having mentors, and he wanted one who was a Christian but also a good business man. This, he admits, is why he first came along to the Fellowship. God blessed him spiritually and financially, and as a result he moved from Oklahoma to New York City in 1960, working as chief accountant for American Airlines. There was no chapter in New York, so with a friend, Fran Nelson, he set about recti- fying this. They met in a Manhattan cafeteria in the basement of a large skyscraper, and before long over 3,000 people would pack it out every Saturday morning.

Tom then got to thinking about Long Island. Lots of people there rarely or never came into the city, so he decided to start another chapter in the area. He organized a Saturday breakfast at the Valley Stream Country Club, and booked for 4,000 places, but on the Thursday it started snowing. Now Tom knew a lot about balance sheets and figures but, coming from Oklahoma, he did not know that when it started snow- ing in New York on Thursday it would not have stopped by Saturday. Only around 1,600 people came – for him, very disappointing – and, being an accountant, he knew the finances would not add up. Up to that time he had not taken offerings in the chapter, but that morning he changed his mind. Even so, the expenses were still not covered. But as Tom was walking out a man came up to him and said, 'I want to take care of your printing and mailing costs.' Fifty cents was left over after the restaurant had been paid!

With both chapters flourishing, Tom decided to look at other areas of the city. Staten Island was next, but they could only find a restaurant that seated about 300, and as twice that many turned up they had to have two sessions. Once that chapter was going, he turned his attention to New Jersey, where another was started. Like so many of the Full Gospel business men, Tom sees the possibilities of bringing together men and women from the business world with visible expressions of God's power to change lives.

Also among early members was Orval Brooks,[2] the owner of a fire alarm communication system company in California. He had been brought up in a Christian home and regularly attended church. But something was missing in his life. For a long time everything went well with the business, but when it started to go downhill he did not know how to deal with it. Orval thought that God wanted to teach him something by bringing adverse circumstances along. A friend invited him to an FGBMFI men's weekend, and for the first time he heard God's word preached in a positive, powerful way. A little later, in July, he attended an FGBMFI convention in San Francisco; the speaker suddenly pointed to the back, where Orval was sitting, and said, 'There's a man in a white sweater for whom the Lord has a word. God will reconcile your life and put you in His perfect will, and before this year is out you'll stand and say, "Glory to God, I'm in the will of the Lord!".' Orval did not know what the will of God was, but by December he had been given a huge contract in Los Angeles, the largest fire alarm job in the city. They did more business in six months than they had ever done in one year. The Holy Spirit had shown him the power of the word of God and how to live it out in all aspects of his life. In the year following, Orval was instrumental in opening the Downey chapter.

Kansas City business man Bill Phipps[3] was converted through attending FGBMFI meetings and then reading Pat Boone's story, yet for the six years following his conversion he could not share his testimony – in fact he could never bring himself to speak in public. One night, while Bill was in the city of Jerusalem, Jesus came to him and showed him speaking in front of huge crowds of people. On his return home, still convinced he could not do this, Bill received a phone call from Jim Webb, the president of the Heart of America chapter of FGBMFI, inviting him to give his testimony during a Saturday morning breakfast at the Holiday Inn. A definite 'no' was on Bill's lips when the vision in Jerusalem came into his mind and, much to his own surprise, he found himself saying he would do it. That morning saw the largest group of business men ever gathered at that time for an FGBMFI breakfast in Kansas City; some people went only to try and make fun of Bill, knowing the kind of life he had led before becoming a Christian. Bill wept as he shared how Jesus had changed his life at the age of 50, and after he had finished many of those who had come to mock him were among the large number who received Jesus into their lives and were filled with the Holy Spirit. A large number of those who responded remained active members of the Full Gospel Business Men's Fellowship.

Part of the ministry of Bill and his wife Marti was working among drug addicts and prostitutes, running a drop-in centre. Having spent a lot of his time before becoming a Christian in gambling joints and 'dives', Bill knew how to make the place look attractive to the people they wanted to reach. After a couple of years they were being carefully watched by narcotic agents, who thought they must be pushing drugs when all the time they were pushing Jesus. One night, an agent was in their place watching a guy he rightly thought was a drug pusher. The agent listened intently to the conversation between the young man and Bill. It was all about Jesus. Instead of arresting the young man, this agent became a Christian, and two weeks later drove a bus round Kansas City picking up drug pushers and taking them to hear Nicky Cruz share his testimony at a Full Gospel Business

Men's meeting. Nicky Cruz was himself a former drug addict and his powerful testimony caused many of those in the meeting to turn their lives over to Jesus.

The Fellowship also provided the opportunity for Christians to invite ministers along to meetings. It was good for them to sit back, relax and enjoy hearing testimonies of how God was working in the business of changing lives. John Steitz, a minister in New Jersey, had many powerful business men in his congregation, but neither he nor they knew how to manoeuvre the church into the mainstream of God's work.[4] A friend of John's, working for his PhD, got involved in a doctoral paper on the subject 'Exactly what happened on the day of Pentecost?' One day he rang John and said there was a group of people called the Full Gospel Business Men's Fellowship International who met regularly at a restaurant in New York City. As he had nothing better to do, John said he would join his friend and go over. Having been concerned for a long time about the renewal of the Spirit, and having read that Martin Luther believed the Church had lost the gifts of the Spirit, John prayed: 'Lord, if the Holy Spirit is descending upon the Church today, then He brings with Him true love. Unless I see love today, Lord, I will not believe.'

When John and his friend arrived at the door of the restaurant, they were greeted by one of the friendliest men he had ever met. Since John was wearing his 'collar', they were taken to a large table reserved for clergymen. Across the table was an elderly priest of the Episcopal Church whose radiance was overwhelming. To his left sat a Roman Catholic friar of the Franciscan order, bubbling over with enthusiasm. Next to him was a very distinguished gentleman who introduced himself as a Baptist preacher. Other ministers were from the Presbyterian and Lutheran churches. What struck John was that these 'men of the cloth', from varied denominational backgrounds, had one thing in common. They were all deeply in love with Jesus Christ. Another strange thing that he had never previously witnessed, despite having marched for civil rights, was when a white man threw his arms around a black man and hugged him. He had never experienced that kind of love before. Later he learned that the white man came from Montgomery, Alabama.

Before the meeting was over, God had answered all John's prayers, filled him with the Holy Spirit and completely changed his outlook. John later resigned his pulpit and became the first European Liaison for the FGBMFI with offices in The Hague, Holland. God then gave him the opportunity to preach in 55 countries on three continents for Jesus and the Spirit-filled life.

One of the most remarkable men to become active in the Fellowship, Dr James E. Johnson, a black American, has a list of 'firsts' that are mind-blowing. To give but a sample:

- first member of the black race to become a commissioned warrant officer in the Unites States Marine Corps
- first member of the black race to retire as an officer of the naval service
- first member of the black race to be appointed to a governor's cabinet – director of the Department of Veterans' Affairs for the state of California under Governor Ronald Reagan
- first member of the black race to become director of the Department of Veterans' Affairs in the state of California
- first member of the black race to be appointed vice chairman of the US Civil Service Commission – appointed by the President of the United States
- first member of the black race to run for the United States Senate from the state of California
- first member of the black race to represent the President and the United States in the Philippines to commemorate with the Philippine Government the fall of Bataan

- first member of the black race to write over $1 million worth of insurance in his first 2½ months in the insurance business.
- first member of the black race to inspect the United States Naval Fleet in the Atlantic as the Assistant Secretary of the Navy
- first member of the black race to be honoured by a foreign government as Assistant Secretary of the Navy
- first member of the black race to commission a major ship, the *USS California*

These represent only a few of his outstanding achievements. He has received eight academic degrees and nearly 800 awards for outstanding achievement and significant service to his country at home and abroad. Since he entered the Marines he has been fighting for the rights of the black peoples of America. His eldest son was the first black boy to go to a white school in Washington DC in 1953, protected by four policemen. One thing that comes over very clearly with 'Johnny' Johnson, as he is generally known, is his refusal to compromise. Whether on racial issues or Christian principles, he would stand his ground whatever the consequences. Dr Johnson's father, who was 6 feet 9 inches tall, weighed 275 pounds, and lived to be 104, was a Christian who instilled his beliefs in God, justice and love, into his son. These, along with unshakeable determination, were to be the foundation for his success.

Although he had heard of the FGBMFI, Johnny Johnson thought they were, in his words, a 'cooky' outfit to be avoided at all costs. However, the men of the Full Gospel, who believed he should be one of them, didn't give up easily. One day, having written up insurance for 300 employees of a plastic manufacturing company, Johnny told the boss, Al, that he wanted a cheque for $37,000 that would not bounce.

The accountant brought in a cheque made payable to Prudential Insurance and Johnny reached out for it. Before he could get hold of the cheque, Al took it, put it in his pocket and said he would hand it over if Johnny would go to a businessman's meeting with him. Not realising what Al meant, and thinking he could get more business out of it, Johnny agreed to go. As they pulled into the car park he saw guys outside the restaurant hugging each other and said that there was no way he was going in. When it came to the crunch of getting the business and the cheque or not, he decided to go in and sit at the back, 'and don't let any of those guys touch me!'

The speaker was a little guy, so skinny that if he turned sideways he would vanish. He was holding onto the lectern and shaking as he told the audience he had been fasting for 40 days. Johnny thought he was stupid until all of a sudden this guy sounded off and said, 'There is a man here with too many degrees and the Lord wants him.' Johnny turned to Al and said, 'You told him I was coming.' Al denied this and then suddenly the guy was pointing at Johnny and said, 'The Lord wants you.' All he wanted to do was get out of the place but a hand touched him on the shoulder. He thought at first it was Al, but it was the little guy, and then in Johnny's words, 'The light went out for me and I heard them saying, "We've got him, praise the Lord!"' He experienced the baptism of the Holy Spirit with speaking in tongues, something in which he had not previously believed. When he got up off the floor his whole attitude towards the people had changed and he felt love, *agape* love, for all the men there. His wife, Juanita said she knew he was different the minute he walked into their home. And of course, he got his cheque!

Shortly after this, Johnny became an International Director for the Fellowship and went to Washington as Under Secretary for the Navy. He thought he could get everybody in

Washington born again in two weeks and could not understand why people would not want to be part of the FGBMFI. First, he started a chapter in Washington, which he ran for 19 years and every four years held a breakfast to celebrate the President's inauguration. 16,000 people came to the first one, and numbers had to be limited to 9,000 in succeeding years. Johnny is now looking to open a chapter in every state capital to be held on the same Saturday morning as the Washington breakfast and from there, to open one in every mayoral town. Who can doubt, given the man's achievements, that with the help of the Holy Spirit, it will happen?

Another important area of work for the FGBMFI in the United States was in prisons. Andrew Kaminski had been a successful businessman but ended up in jail because of a technicality over an amount of a few dollars owed to the government. He was a Christian before this happened but it was in Lomoc Federal Prison, California that he came into an experience of the Holy Spirit. Every Monday evening the FGBMFI came into the prison and conducted a regular chapter meeting. The chapter was set up in exactly the same way as those on the outside where a couple of men would give short testimonies and then a main speaker. Each week would see between 70 to 100 men coming along.

On one occasion as Andrew and his friend George were on their way to the chapter meeting, they passed the cell of a prisoner who was lying on his bunk, and felt they should invite him to go with them. He refused, saying he had heard about them and didn't believe in anything they were doing. Then he paused for a moment and said, 'If your God is so powerful why don't you pray for my alarm clock sitting on that ledge, and maybe you can make it work.' Andrew looked at George and asked what he thought. George was all for praying and so they did. Within a moment the alarm clock, one of those large round ones, started ticking. So impressed was the prisoner that he jumped off the bunk and said he would go with them. That night he decided to turn his life over to Jesus and as a result, became a different person. Andrew Kaminski is now the World Director for FGBMFI Prison Work.

This short testimony shows how powerful a tool the *Voice* magazine can be. A truck driver from San Lorenzo, California, wrote in to the Editor with the following story:

> I stopped along the highway to check my equipment and found this magazine, *Voice*, in the weeds. I am now a born again Christian (three years) after 49 years without committing my life to Jesus. I would like an application to become a member.[5]

One of Demos' competitors in the dairy business, but a brother in Christ, was Norman Frost. One day he called Demos and asked him to come and pray for his grandson, Sam. Rose and Demos left immediately for the Children's Hospital of Orange County some twenty or so miles away. Sam was 13 years old and afflicted with Reye's Syndrome – which causes the brain to swell dangerously inside the skull. Doctors didn't expect him to live through the night.

As soon as they walked into the hospital room, the heart of Demos went out to the boy. He was screaming, and rolling on his bed in excruciating pain so that the nurses had to strap him down by his hands and feet to prevent him from hurting himself. Demos reached out to touch his face but his head jerked so violently that he couldn't keep his hand there. Finally, he lightly tapped the boy's forehead as he tossed and screamed and suddenly, Sam relaxed. Demos put his hands on his head and prayed simply in the name of Jesus that the Lord would touch the Reye's Syndrome, reduce the pressure, heal the affliction and enable Sam to be normal. With that, young Sam drifted off to sleep. The next morning he awoke free from pain and completely healed. Any possibilities of permanent damage from the stress on his brain were ruled out when, a few years later, Sam went on to be a straight A university student and a computer wiz.[6]

An agnostic businessman in British Columbia turned on his TV one night and heard another businessman's testimony of God's life-changing power. This businessman not only applied it to his life, but became the president of a chapter in his home town. The programme he had seen was one hosted by Demos Shakarian, 'Good News Tonight', which was sold to many television stations across the country. In the early seventies, the programmes began to be shown in Hawaii.

Harold Shiraki was the first man to ring in because of the Hawaiian broadcasts.[7] Of Japanese parentage, he had been raised to work hard, consider others and respect authority. His father had Parkinson's disease and when he became too ill to work, the older children left school to support the family. Harold, however, was able to continue his education and was the first in the family to graduate from high school. He moved to Honolulu where he worked hard and saved money, only to have it taken away from him by men he trusted. Nominally, Harold was a Buddhist and relied on faith in human effort and decency, not in God. He had joined the Episcopal church because it seemed to offer freedom from the fears of his childhood religion and now he spoke to a clergyman about his loss of money. He was counselled against taking the men to court and advised to forget it. That Harold could not do. He stopped eating, seeing friends, and allowed the hatred to build up inside him.

He decided to borrow a gun from a friend and commit suicide. Sunday was the day he planned to do it. On that day, his wife begged him to go to church but he refused. She then begged him to turn on the television and at least watch a ball game to take his mind away from his problems. To make sure his wife suspected nothing, he turned on the set but the channel was showing two men talking. So distracted was he that at first he could not take in what they were saying except he noticed they were the happiest-looking people he had ever seen. Harold tried to concentrate on the words and as he did a strange peace settled over him. When the programme ended, a telephone number was listed for people to ring and he quickly found himself talking to the president of the Honolulu chapter of FGBMFI. He was told that Jesus loved him, knew about his situation and that He was the answer to Harold's problems.

Harold never got his money back but a new life began for him from that Sunday. Among the first people to respond to the change in her son, was his mother. Realizing that there was a power greater than that of the spirits she'd been appeasing, the whole family burned the images and shrines they formerly worshipped.

As well as these programmes that touched people like Harold in Honolulu, FGBMFI also made TV and video recordings of Convention meetings. One of the most outstanding of these was 'Good News America' featuring the 1976 World Convention. Speakers such as Kathryn Kuhlman, Rex Humbard, Pat Boone and Oral Roberts captivated the audience and viewers.

An electrifying message, probably the most powerful of that Convention, was preached by Oral Roberts. Entitled, 'The Fourth Man', this concerned the three young men in the Old Testament cast into a furnace for refusing to bow down to King Nebuchadnezzar. Looking into the furnace the king was amazed to see not only the three young men apparently unharmed, but with them a fourth man, 'like the Son of God.' Roberts then went on to give a recitation concerning Jesus throughout the Old and New Testaments. Starting off in Genesis where he described Him as the 'seed of the woman' and in Exodus, 'the Passover lamb', he went through every book of the Bible, finally coming to the triumphant conclusion that the Fourth Man was Jesus of Nazareth, King of kings and Lord of lords.

FOUR

Becoming International

From the outset of the Fellowship, Demos had been convinced by the Holy Spirit that it should spread around the world. Once men caught the vision God had given him, not only did it spread like wildfire throughout the States, the members also looked to new horizons.

The first overseas chapter was established in Johannesburg, South Africa, as early as 1955 but it was not until business men from Toronto, Canada, invited Demos to come and introduce the Fellowship to that country that a sense of excitement was generated among the leadership that the Fellowship was now truly going international.

Once again, leading healing evangelists were involved in helping take FGBMFI to new countries of the world. In his Argentinian crusade, Tommy Hicks presented President Peron with a Bible and a copy of *Voice* magazine. He also visited Russia, Switzerland and Finland where he constantly encouraged men to become involved in the Fellowship

Within a few years, new chapters were started as far away as India, Hong Kong, Singapore, China, Korea, Japan, Switzerland, Germany, a second chapter in Cape Town,

South Africa, and, nearer to America, Haiti, Cuba and Mexico. Many leading evangelists were involved, including Hicks, Sam Todd and T.L. Osborne, and members of the Fellowship such as Miner Arganbright and Thomas Nickel, the man who, at the very beginning, gave his printing press to print *Voice* magazine.

Cuba, so close to the United States, was worlds apart in so many ways following Fidel Castro's successful coup in 1959. A small group including Demos and Rose went over to the island; it was to be Demos' first visit to a Communist country. The following story is one he shared many times, and it indicates how sensitive he was to the Holy Spirit. The group was staying in the Havana Hilton, the place which Castro had made his headquarters. In the early hours of the morning, Demos felt impelled to get dressed and go down to the restaurant where, he believed, he would have the opportunity to speak to Fidel Castro. Naturally speaking, that was an impossibility: for one thing, Castro was always surrounded by armed guards and, anyway, according to the waiter in the restaurant he would not be in that night.

Demos believed God. He told the waiter that when Castro came in he was to tell him that Demos was a dairyman from California and would like to speak with him. The waiter was a little non-plussed, thinking that his information was wrong, and he asked Demos if someone had told him that Castro would be there that night. Knowing there was little point in saying the Holy Spirit had given the information, Demos just said yes, someone had told him. Still unable to accept this, the waiter told Demos that Castro never came into the restaurant after ten o'clock; this was at nearly three in the morning.

Having waited for some considerable time, Demos was beginning to think he had heard wrongly, so he picked up the bill for the ice-cream he had eaten and walked over to pay.

Even as the change was being counted out, he heard heavy footsteps outside, and suddenly through the door came a group of men in fatigues. In the centre was Fidel Castro.

So impressed was the waiter that Demos had the correct information that he went over to Castro, who had sat down and ordered food, and whispered to him. Castro looked up and beckoned Demos to come over to his table. Surrounded by guns, Demos sat down and chatted to this enigmatic man, even making him laugh. He took the opportunity, when asked why he was there, to share about the Fellowship and how they wanted to get to know Cubans who were working in a similar way, and also about what the Holy Spirit was doing among people like themselves in other countries. The two men talked for over half an hour, until they were rudely interrupted by a local business man who wanted to complain about what Castro was doing to the nightclubs of Cuba. Castro turned to Demos, saying he was glad he had come. 'I wish ...' he began – and at this point the conversation was terminated because trouble was beginning to brew with the nightclub owner. Demos often shared about how he wondered what Castro had wished, but only God knows that.

Rarely is God's Kingdom extended without cost, be that family, financial or in other ways. That always applied in the Full Gospel Business Men's Fellowship International. When FGBMFI men took part in an airlift, they paid all their own expenses and often had to take their holiday time as well. This was the case in 1960, when a group of men took off for Haiti and the Silvio Cato Stadium in Port-au-Prince.

The meetings ... exceeded the wildest dreams of the planners, drawing twenty-three thousand persons to the stadium the first night and soon overflowing to thirty-five thousand persons. Despite opposition from voodoo priests, and the dubious support of Duvalier (the president of Haiti), the campaign continued with increasing force. After the sensational healing of a blind boy, the meetings overflowed the stadium grounds. On the last night of the stadium, over ten thousand persons came forward for salvation. After three weeks ended, it was estimated that over a hundred thousand had been saved.[1]

In Canada, it was February 1960 when the Fellowship was officially constituted in that country. Sixty-six men sat down in Hemstead's Restaurant, Toronto, where they were ignited by the fire of the Holy Spirit. A Toronto business man, Larry Snelgrove, had met Demos and other American leaders in 1955 and they had earlier held a banquet in Toronto at which the Fellowship was introduced to the people of Canada. Now they were getting serious. The need for sharing fellowship, coming together with people of like minds, and winning men and women for Jesus were the factors motivating these and other men around the world.

In succeeding years, Canada saw tens of thousands of lives touched through the vehicle of the FGBMFI. Thousands of breakfast, luncheon and banquet meetings later, they are able to report that the power of Jesus Christ has healed bodies, minds, emotions, spirits, families and businesses, from one end of the nation to the other.

Television also featured in the work as they filmed *Good News* in Canada, and the showing of this programme brought thousands of people to a commitment of their lives to Jesus. One of the greatest areas of success was in new Chinese chapters opening in Toronto and Vancouver. These saw between 400 and 600 attending, with well over half of these being non-Christians. The National Board not only set specific goals for expansion, but also sent out a challenge to every member in Canada to set aside one day a week to fast and pray for the ministry of FGBMFI, and as a result they have seen God move in amazing ways.

When friends asked questions such as, 'How could you take such a risk? What on earth made you do it? I would never employ anyone like that!', Grant Bailey, owner of Bailey's Sports Store, would probably have replied, 'Because Jesus has changed my life and He can do the same for anyone.' The issue here was a man called Ernie Hollands. Brought up in a very poor two-room shack in the slum area of Halifax, Nova Scotia, Canada, Ernie never saw the inside of a church, and no one had ever put their arms around him and said he was loved. He was taught how to steal – it was called 'survival'.

From the age of 12, when he was placed in a reform institution, Ernie Hollands was to spend 25 years 'inside'. He became a hardened and habitual criminal, a constant escapee who eventually became so institutionalized he could not survive outside prison. During his last sentence, Ernie started to make fish flies as a way of passing the time. So good were these flies that the making of them grew into a profitable occupation. Ernie started making contacts with sports stores, which is where Grant Bailey comes into the story. He owned such a store in Pembrook, Ontario. At first Grant wasn't sure he wanted to buy the flies. However, he decided to acknowledge Ernie's letter, and at the end of his reply told him about how important it was to know Jesus, the only one who could save us from ourselves. Later he sent Ernie a Bible and shared how he had only recently become a Christian. Grant was the first person ever to tell Ernie about God and His Son Jesus, who loved Ernie and had died for his sins.

Ernie started reading the Bible, thinking it might be a way to impress the guards, but very soon it began to get hold of him and he found he was reading 15 to 20 chapters a day. He found he didn't hate any more, had stopped arguing and started making friends! One night a miracle took place in his cell. Instead of just praying words, he prayed from the depths of his soul, and Ernie saw Jesus. He came into Ernie's cell, put His hands on his shoulders, and said, 'Ernie Hollands, your slate is wiped clean.'

The second miracle was when Ernie walked free, 23 months later, three and a half years before the end of his sentence. Outside the prison, waiting with a van to transport 34 cartons of fish flies, was Grant Bailey. He had opened his home and had a job waiting for Ernie in his store. Grant was a member of the FGBMFI, and giving this opportunity to Ernie was his contribution to spreading the Gospel. Eventually, Ernie was receiving so many invitations from FGBMFI chapters, churches, schools and television that he had to give up his employment at the store and spend his life travelling, sharing his testimony and helping to build up the prison ministry of the Fellowship in Canada. Many people there, and in other parts of the world, got to know the name of Ernie Hollands. Very few remember the name of Grant Bailey, but it is laymen like him being obedient to God that make the Ernie Hollands of this world possible.

A young man called Ray Barnett,[2] originally from Northern Ireland, moved to Canada in the late 1950s and became the catalyst for one of the most significant airlifts of the Fellowship. Like so many of his generation, Ray had left Ireland to go to London. There, he felt the call of God on his life and decided that meant he should be a minister. He started his training with one of the mainline churches, but two problems stood in his way. One was dyslexia, which meant he found it difficult to express his ideas in written form. Second, the teaching he was getting seemed to dismiss so much of what he believed and knew about God – no room for ideas about the Virgin Birth or the baptism of the Holy Spirit and speaking in tongues. Earlier in his life, he had had two other serious problems: stammering, and passing out if he ever had to stand to do something in front of people. These latter two had been miraculously healed when he had been baptized in the Holy Spirit.

By 1961, he felt he was still not fulfilling God's call on his life. That year he went for an interview with a leading travel agent in Calgary and put a startling proposal to them. What would they think of a person like him handling nothing but religious and missionary travel? It would, he assured them, bring in a lot of business as well as providing a valuable service to the church community. After a slight hesitation they accepted his proposal, and it was through this work that he first came across the FGBMFI. He attended the 1962 convention in Seattle during the World's Fair, and God sowed the seed of an ambitious project in his heart – not just an airlift to the UK, but one that would incorporate a massive convention in London. Meanwhile he began working for the Fellowship locally, opening a chapter in Calgary. He also became the youngest International Director of the Fellowship.

Jerry Jensen, editor of *Voice* magazine, was the speaker at the second Calgary breakfast meeting. Ray decided that he would discuss the project with him. He took Jerry to the world-famous resort of Banff and Lake Louise, and as they travelled through the spectacular scenery of mountains and forests they spoke about the unique way in which God had led each of them. Later that afternoon, relaxing in the resort's hot springs, Ray shared his idea of flying two or three jets filled with business men to the UK. As he talked, his vision and excitement grew. He visualized a convention in London that would reach thousands of people with the Gospel.

Although he was excited by the idea, Jerry was also a little guarded. An airlift had been successfully organized to Haiti, but this was on an altogether different scale. As soon as he got back to Los Angeles, Jerry discussed the idea with Demos, and later that week phoned Ray to come down and discuss plans. Making an appointment with Demos was not easy. Always busy, he had agreed to see the two men between 11.30 and 11.45 following the Saturday morning breakfast meeting at Clifton's Cafeteria. Fifteen minutes to discuss such a massive project! Ray knew that was impossible. But once Demos started to listen to this young man's vision, he decided to give over the entire day to discussion of the airlift and, by midnight, the three men had come to a decision.

Not only would there be an airlift to London, with a convention, but they decided to make it the World Convention. Ray was given the role of convention co-ordinator, and he travelled thousands of miles in the United States and abroad, aiming to inspire business men throughout the world to come to the convention in London.[3]

FIVE

Spiritual Blitz on the UK

Destination London

Saturday 20 November 1965 was truly a 'red-letter day' for the Full Gospel Business Men's Fellowship. In three airports, Los Angeles, New York and Chicago, groups of people waited to send off their friends and families to London, with their prayers and blessings. In the lobby of the Los Angeles International Airport about a thousand people gathered, among whom were well-known figures such as Nicky Cruz and Demos and Rose Shakarian, waiting to board the Scandinavian Airways jet.

Never before, and probably not since, had that airport lounge witnessed such a scene. The electrifying presence of God was sensed by everyone. Five ex-drug addicts stood up and sang, 'We've come this far by faith', while other men spoke about the miracles that had enabled them to be part of this historic event.

At the opposite side of the country, at Kennedy International Airport, New York, another group stood waiting to board a jet, looking anxiously for a helicopter to land with Judge Kermit Bradford, who had been delayed in Atlanta. With only minutes to spare, he joined the 143 waiting passengers. And in the city of Chicago, 127 people boarded a third jet, sent off with songs and prayers by a host of well-wishers. Among these were the Rev. Derek Prince and his wife and Steve Shakarian, whose father had already left from Los Angeles.

Richard Shakarian believed that the 1965 airlift to the UK was significant largely because of the world position that country held in terms of the Commonwealth. Whatever hit the media headlines in London was rapidly spread over the wires world-wide. Hardly surprising that when the UK public opened their morning newspapers to read headlines such as: 'Millionaire Demos Brings Deliverance to the Beatniks of Britain', 'Big Business in Soho', and 'Full Gospel in London', the stories were picked up.

Six days before the planes left America, the *Sunday Express* published an article that had been gathering dust for six months. It was entitled 'The people who "speak" in a language they do not know'. It was not newspaper policy in those days to deal with such issues, especially not a full-page spread. Asking the question, 'Has one of the mysteries of the early Church been revived in our modern age?' the writer, David Sanders, quoted the passage from Acts chapter 2 which graphically describes the day of Pentecost, when the Holy Spirit was poured out as promised in Joel 2:28–9. The article was neither superficial nor denigrating, but gave the subject thoughtful and open-minded consideration.

The timing of this publication received comment from many other press writers over the next three weeks because of the events connected with the airlift. The reason for this was the importance placed on this experience by the FGBMFI and the openness with which it was spoken about by the men and women from America who were interviewed by the press.

Nicky Cruz was one of a number on the airlift who had been delivered from drug addiction when they turned their lives over to Jesus. These were the men described by the *Sun* as 'Mr Shakarian's shock troops'. Going out into the Soho area to speak to the rebels of the day, 'beatniks' and drug addicts, they did not go to condemn their lifestyle but were living proof of the power of the Holy Spirit to break addiction and bring life and hope to an individual. From a report on some twenty 'youthful derelicts', each of whom had made a decision to give Jesus a chance to work in their lives, a rather amusing story surfaced. George Gardner, a car dealer from New York, hired two rooms in the Hilton and moved all the furniture into one, covering the floor of the other with canvas. Then he hired two barbers to cut the long hair of these newly 'born again' ex-drug addicts. By the time they eventually finished, the floor was covered in hair to a depth of almost six inches. A bath and new suit of clothes followed, turning them into smart young people. Not the way things would be handled today, but the 1960s were very different!

However, that was not the end of the story. A very concerned hotel manager rang Demos and told him they would all have to vacate the hotel immediately. Demos could not get any sense out of him, so a group of men went down to discuss the matter. The manager was quite distraught and adamant that they should leave. He accused them of bringing large numbers of beatniks into his hotel and then hiding them in their rooms. They took him up to the room where the 'clean-up' operation was taking place, and he could not believe his eyes. Needless to say, he relented and allowed everyone to stay.

One example of so many young people in Soho was Johnny. Having got himself into trouble once in his home town of Newcastle, he discovered that people expected trouble from him all the time. He had been involved in theft and was sent to a correctional institute; afterwards, he found it impossible to fit back into school, where he was constantly under suspicion. Like many others, he ended up hanging around London's 'square mile of evil', an angry young man. Johnny saw his former associates accept Jesus and undergo not only a spiritual transformation but also a physical one. He eventually decided to try the former, but he was determined to hang on to his long hair – it was his badge of disdain for society. Although he had decided to give his life to Jesus, deep within his anger and bitterness were tearing him apart. A few days later, he received the baptism of the Holy Spirit, setting him free and enabling him to forgive. The next day, with only a fraction of hesitation, he allowed the barber to cut the first huge handful of hair.

Inevitably, this aspect of the airlift's work caught the imagination of the press more than any other. They followed the teams wherever they went, photographing and interviewing the new converts. There was, of course, a good deal of scepticism, and Demos Shakarian was asked how genuine he believed the conversions were. 'Of course, we can be fooled,' he said, 'even taken for a ride by some of the people we help. We expect that. Others attempt to change their lives but slip back into their old ways despite our help. But if only one person here starts a completely new life – and in doing so shows an example to many others – well, then every cent of what we spend here and every minute of our time in Britain will have been worth it.' As the press pointed out, the convention in the hotel and air fares alone cost about £85,000 (in Britain at that time, the average wage would be about £1,000 a year), all to be met out of the delegates' pockets. But one fact was very difficult to explain away. The ex-drug addicts showed their arms to the reporters, who saw that the needle marks had miraculously healed and that they were completely free of any withdrawal symptoms.

Press reporters, Granada Television, BBC Radio, local policemen and even Scotland Yard descended on the Hilton

Hotel and Soho to see what was going on. They heard in amazement that one man had donated enough money to send several young men on the trip, all former drug addicts but healed and filled with the Holy Spirit. Among those who went into Soho with the team was a narcotics officer from Scotland Yard. Like many doctors and others who worked with addicts, he believed that it was impossible for anyone hooked on drugs ever to be totally freed from the habit. What he saw was addicts responding to the call to give their lives to Jesus and being immediately baptized in the Holy Spirit, speaking in tongues. He saw their lives transformed as they stopped using drugs without any withdrawal symptoms, so that they were able to return to work. Not surprisingly, he was one of three London policemen who also became Christians that week.

'Beatniks and Soho' were not the only headlines about the airlift. In the rather more sober *Church of England Newspaper*, under the title 'Full Gospel Men in Church House' were equally remarkable stories. The first public meeting was scheduled for Westminster Chapel on the Wednesday evening, but the day started with a seven o'clock prayer meeting followed by a breakfast meeting at eight o'clock, and after-service sessions of prayer with those wanting salvation or baptism in the Holy Spirit. The opening session was a little stiff at first, as the Americans and British felt strange with each other, but when they began to sing, the Spirit of the Lord began to move. It was a truly international and interdenominational gathering, and one minister exclaimed, 'For twenty years I have been a pastor, but never have I experienced a crusade where there was such a spirit of unity as prevailed in the spiritual airlift to London.'

Long before Ray Barnett had been led to organize this convention, God had been preparing men in the UK. The 1950s had seen the great crusade at Haringey when Billy

Graham and his team, together with many churches, held a three-months' campaign. It is impossible to quantify the results fully. Thousands came forward to make a commitment to Jesus Christ, many becoming ministers themselves. The effect was ongoing, as church congregations throughout the country began to experience a growing desire for a deeper experience in the Christian life. This was not confined to any specific church or denomination, nor to any particular part of the land. A man who was to become a member of the FGBMFI, Andy Milliken, wrote in his book *From the Kwai to the Kingdom*, 'A vision was beginning to surface for outreach activities, and a new compassion stirred for other Christians wherever they worshipped, and for those who did not know the Lord. One of the most important foundations of the Full Gospel Business Men's Fellowship is its interdenominationalism, men and women being encouraged to stay in their churches.'[1]

Arising from the success of the Haringey Crusade, a monthly evening fellowship meal was held at the YMCA in Tottenham Court Road. About 70 people, mostly business men but with some pastors and evangelists, would meet to seek ways of sharing the Gospel using modern techniques. Unfortunately, despite many good ideas, nothing specific came out of these meetings until one night when a pastor from south London stood up and made a suggestion. Was it not time they stopped telling God what they wanted to do and start listening to what God had to say? So simple!

A regular lunchtime prayer meeting in the heart of the city for business men was what they believed God was telling them to do. This was held in Fleet Street; it received a tremendous anointing from the Holy Spirit over the next few years and became known world-wide. People gave up their lunch in order not to miss what God was doing in that prayer group. The Fleet Street group received many letters asking about the renewal in Great Britain, particularly from America, and it was from that country that an unusual request came in 1965. They were asked if they could arrange a 'steering committee' for a group of Americans who wanted to visit Britain in November. Americans! The group were, to say the least, cautious, even sceptical. It took considerable persuasion before several of them agreed to form such a team. Although few people in Britain had heard of the FGBMFI, those comprising the steering committee were prepared to step out in faith. These included the Rev. Michael Harper, Andy Milliken, then an advertising and public relations consultant, the Rev. Ernest Walton-Lewsey, Director of the London Embankment Mission, and William (Bill) Thompson, a Savile Row tailor, who chaired the group. Other men were drawn in to help with the enormous organization of such a venture.

Bill Thompson was a key figure in God's plan for the FGBMFI in Britain. He visited the United States twice a year to sell his hand-made suits, and while there would take the opportunity to visit churches and religious communities. His contact with the FGBMFI came about in a remarkable way through Lee Buck. Lee worked for the New York Life Insurance Company, supervising more than 10,000 agents and 350 offices in the United States and Canada. He was also a director of FGBMFI.

In the middle of a very busy day in his Madison Avenue office, Lee received a telephone call from an Englishman. It went something like this:

'Mr Buck, my name is Bill Thompson and I am a friend of Bob Kuenzle. I just thought I would ring you up.'

'Well, Mr Thompson, what can I do for you?'

'Nothing, really. I just wanted to say hello.'

Apart from mentioning the name of his hotel, this was the entire conversation. After a few moments of looking at the work on his desk, Lee began to think about this rather odd exchange. He decided he had probably been rather abrupt.

If Bill Thompson was a friend of Bob's then he must be a Christian, and Lee had better quickly return the call. As soon as they were connected he asked, 'Mr Thompson, are you a Christian?'

From this rather inauspicious beginning came the connection between the Fleet Street group and the FGBMFI, as well as a life-long friendship. Bill later met Demos and other members in the United States, and in this God completed another part of His 'jig-saw puzzle' so that the right men were available at the right time.

Ray Barnett and Jerry Jensen flew to London a couple of weeks before the airlift to join the men who were dealing with the final arrangements. It was an enormous task. Hundreds of hotel reservations had to be made for those coming from America on the three chartered jets; meeting places had to be booked as well as flights and accommodation for those going on to Europe. In addition, there were hundreds of invitations for teams of individuals to go and speak in churches, colleges, prisons, factories and homes throughout the country. There was such a demand for speakers and seminars to discuss forming FGBMFI chapters that many of the men involved had hardly slept for days. However, everyone was encouraged by the co-operation of ministers and the friendliness of those contacted for help, including some MPs. As Bill Thompson was to exclaim, 'This isn't a convention! This is an appointment with God!'

As Ray watched the first plane taxi to a halt that November morning, he experienced eagerness, mild impatience and a sense of relief, as well as disbelief. Had he had any idea of what was to follow, he probably could not have taken it in.

One of the pilots probably felt a sense of relief too. At 33,000 feet over the Atlantic, an irregularity was detected. Both pilot and co-pilot were baffled as there was no visible engineering or hydraulic reason for the fault, so they asked the flight engineer to take a quick look at the rear of the plane. Walking down the long gangway, he was taken aback to find no one in any of the passenger seats in the forward section. The reason for the problem soon became clear. Entering the rear cabin, he found all the passengers gathered together, worshipping God. As politely as possible, he ordered them back to their original seats, saying that otherwise they were likely to meet their Maker sooner than envisaged!

The journey across the Atlantic had produced some wonderful testimonies. One man, Miles Smith of Kankakee, Illinois, described himself as 80 years young, but unfortunately could not prove that he had ever been born! Determined to be part of the airlift, he drove hundreds of miles across country in wintry weather to find his 90-year-old brother in order to obtain an affidavit acceptable to the Passport Office. Miles had once heard an evangelist say that if you want a blessing from God, you must first make a point of contact. He decided that his would be attending the London convention, where he hoped to receive the baptism of the Holy Spirit. In mid-flight, high over the Atlantic, one of the men walked down the aisle of the plane and said, 'Miles, what about praying for you now?' He placed his arms around him and the Lord immediately filled Miles with His Holy Spirit.

Others told of how God had met their financial needs by providing unexpected overtime, or how contracts that had dragged on for months had suddenly been completed, making finance available. Throughout all three flights, the crew members saw and heard a Christian witness wherever they turned, with people praying, singing and praising the Lord.

Stepping out of the warm plane into the chilly November morning, Rose Shakarian commented how everything looked so strange and different, as if out of a storybook. Many people in the following three weeks clearly wondered what had hit London as the enthusiastic Americans took every opportunity to witness for Jesus.

One of the amazing aspects of the convention was the number of people who went to London not knowing what it was about but feeling impelled by God to be there. Many had never experienced breakfast and luncheon meetings in a hotel, and some thought that perhaps the Hilton was too luxurious. God quite clearly showed one man why the convention wasn't based at an inexpensive small hotel – apart from the size! As he went up to his room on one occasion, an African gentleman in a multi-coloured, richly embroidered robe and turban swept into the lift and returned his greeting with dignity. On being invited to attend the final meeting at the Royal Albert Hall that night, the dignitary very promptly and graciously accepted. As he left the lift, one of the other men gasped, 'Do you know who that is? That's the vice premier of Nigeria!'

On that last day of the convention, two meetings were held in the Royal Albert Hall. In the afternoon Nicky Cruz addressed the young people who packed the hall, and Oral Roberts was the guest speaker in the evening. If ever there was a doubt that the Christians of the UK were open to knowing more of the power of the Holy Spirit, the World Convention, and especially the Saturday evening, dispelled any such claim. The hall, which holds over 5,000 people, was filled to capacity with many thousands more left outside, unable to get in.

It was not the singing or the preaching or even the countless people who responded to the final appeal that made such a deep impression. At the end of his inspiring address, Oral Roberts asked everyone to stand and speak out loud in tongues. Although many people in Britain had experienced baptism in the Holy Spirit, they had never spoken out loud in tongues in a public meeting in this way. The effect was electrifying. One long-time Pentecostal minister described it as a manifestation of God's power that made history. He had never known it happen anywhere before. This, more than anything else, perhaps, was what characterized the FGBMFI among other interdenominational organizations. It experienced, 'that which was spoken of by the prophet Joel: "And it shall come to pass in the last days," saith God, "I will pour of my Spirit upon all flesh; and your sons and your daughters shall prophesy, and your young men shall see visions, and your old men shall dream dreams; and on my servants and on my handmaidens I will pour out in those days of my Spirit."'

During the second week of the trip, delegates were divided into teams, travelling all over Britain and further afield. One group in Newcastle witnessed to approximately 3,000, either in group meetings or by personal ministry. They saw 50 people commit their lives to Jesus Christ, 22 baptized in the Holy Spirit and four miraculously healed. Two people testified to having received the Holy Spirit after reading *Voice* magazine, one a minister of a mission and the other a Baptist minister.

Judge Kermit Bradford had breakfast with some 15 barristers at the Ivanhoe Hotel. The group was led by a Queen's Counsel, Mr Poson. At the other end of the social scale, a doctor from New Mexico witnessed to a young boy of 15 in a snack bar, and he committed his life to Jesus. That alone would have made the doctor's trip worthwhile, but two days later he returned to give the young man, Raymond, a New Testament. At the snack bar he found Raymond witnessing to another young man about Jesus. As he saw the doctor approaching Raymond said, 'Here he comes now. He will finish telling you about Jesus.'

Another team went to Christ College, Cambridge, where students listened intently to the various testimonies. On subsequent evenings, three students became Christians and eight were baptized in the Holy Spirit. Some teams visited cities and towns across Wales, Scotland, the Isle of Wight, Guernsey and Ireland. Other teams moved out into Europe to consolidate and further spread the work of the Fellowship.

When Ray Barnett and Jerry Jensen parted at Heathrow for the homeward journey, Ray turned to his friend and said, 'Jerry, more than ten years ago I left Ireland for the last time. Everyone begged me not to go, and I didn't know what to say to the people. Finally I promised them that if I went to Canada, I'd do something for them I could never do if I stayed in Ireland.' Jerry looked at him quietly for a moment, thinking what a remarkable man this was. 'So,' he said, 'you've kept your promise.'

Had that been all, Ray Barnett's vision of planeloads of men flying out to another country to share the Gospel had more than come to pass. But another vision was also becoming a reality – the vision that God had given Demos, some thirteen years earlier, of how He was going to bring men all over the world back to spiritual life and vitality.

SIX

Catching the Vision

Following such a powerful impact made by the American airlift and the apparent enthusiasm for the aims of the Fellowship, it was surprising that only a few chapters were established. Of these, only Preston and Belfast survived the following ten years. Much thought and discussion has been given to this, and the consensus seems to be that the major reason was the lack of Spirit-filled people in the UK. Not until the charismatic movement had thoroughly taken hold did the FGBMFI see the kind of growth one might have expected after 1965. Somehow, the people had not, as Ray Barnett had dreamed, been able to 'catch the vision'. That was to come later.

In addition to the problem of insufficient men for leadership, the Fellowship was not well organized in the UK. Bill Thompson had been encouraged by the American FGBMFI men into another project that side-tracked him from developing the work of the Fellowship at this time. Lack of communication between the groups in Britain, as well as between them and the States, appears to have been another factor in the early difficulties of the Fellowship.

Originally, a chapter was set up in Belfast in 1957 by Thomas Nickel and Miner Arganbright, along with other men. Their contact in Belfast believed that a chapter in that city would enable them to rise above the narrow-mindedness and denominationalism that prevailed in Northern Ireland. Despite this optimism, virtually nothing more is known about the group, although it was probably due to them that the American *Voice* magazine continued to come to Ireland, paving the way for a tremendous move of God in the coming years.

Billy Burke was one of those who regularly received the American *Voice* and it was in that magazine that he saw the advertisement for the World Convention in London in 1965. He knew without any doubt that he had to be in London for that event. This was the Sunday; the convention started the following Wednesday. Billy rang his cousin, George Allen, a successful business man, to see if he was interested in going. Billy was a Presbyterian elder and George was the co-ordinator for all Protestant faiths of Northern Ireland, a strong conservative evangelical. Interested but cautious, George asked another friend to go with them. In the eyes of many British people at that time, Americans, especially those who came to the UK, were perceived as wealthy. When Billy sat down at the first luncheon meeting, he was first over-whelmed by the knowledge that he was where he should be, right in the presence of God. The second sensation was one almost of disbelief when he learned that the American couple sharing their table had had to borrow the money to come to London. The week following the convention, this couple went over to Ireland at the invitation of George Allen, where they saw tremendous miracles happen and the Belfast chapter was restarted.

In 1966, a chapter was opened in Ballymena, a town ultra-conservative in its Protestantism. Jim Fleming, the chapter president, shook his evangelical friends to the core not only by 'going Pentecostal' but by accepting Roman Catholics into the Fellowship. That was going beyond the pale.

Two significant events preceded the turning point for the UK. In 1974 the men of the Preston chapter were still going on in what they thought was isolation. They had become very discouraged and were on the point of closing the chapter down when God spoke and said, 'Hold on, I am going to bless this work in a mighty way.' Shortly afterwards, a management consultant in Cheshire, Bob Spilman, was crying out to God, believing there was more to Christianity than he had yet experienced. He very soon experienced the baptism in the Holy Spirit, and after receiving a copy of *Voice* magazine wrote off to America to ask if there were any groups in the UK. Early in 1976 he received a Chapter Manual, and by then he had contacted a number of men in his area to come together and pray.

On 24 April 1976, six men came together in Bob's home to start a chapter, two of whom Bob had never met. None of them knew anything at all about the Fellowship, but they believed they should set up a chapter, with officers. On being appointed president, Bob asked what they should do next. The reply was, 'Well, you're the president – you decide!'

At that precise moment the telephone rang. The caller was Phil Israelson, an American phoning from London. He had come to Britain in faith with two other colleagues from the Seattle chapter (one of whom was Steve Lightle, a very significant man for the UK and Europe, as we shall see in Chapter 8). Arriving in London, they had not known what to do, so they prayed and then telephoned a man in Northern Ireland. He had given them the telephone number of the house where the men were meeting. No one knows how he got the number, but God's timing is always perfect.

God was preparing his people all over England, Ireland (both north and south) and Scotland, where in 1977 a convention was held. This had no media-grabbing headlines to herald it, but like the 1965 convention it too became a catalyst not only for change but also for tremendous growth, this time right across the UK and Ireland. The three-day convention in Glasgow was described by many as 'heaven on earth'. A number of Americans who had been involved in 1965 were present, as well as those to whom God had been speaking in the various parts of the UK and Ireland. Many Europeans were also there, and everyone went home with a new enthusiasm to begin or further the work of the Fellowship in their area. The last meeting was electric. Demos had never seen 500 people all dancing before the Lord, and as they sang 'Joy is the flag' many in that place had to reassess their opinion of the 'reserved' British.

The Full Gospel Business Men's Fellowship International became firmly established in the UK and Ireland following the 1977 convention, and it soon became clear that people had caught the vision of what it was all about. The men came forward to establish new chapters and the work grew apace. One of the good things that has become clear over the years is the variety of chapters. Although each one follows a basic format of having a president, vice president (or two), treasurer and secretary, holding regular outreach dinners or breakfasts, sometimes luncheons, the character of each chapter reflects the area and the different people involved. Some are more formal while others have a more casual evening. Whatever its individual features, the aim of each chapter remains constant – to reach men and women for Jesus, to bring healing and deliverance to those in need and to encourage fellowship and unity among the many denominations that make up the Body of Christ.

So many testimonies portray the outworking of the Fellowship. Peter Spreckley, a lawyer by profession and senior partner in his firm, seemed to have everything that counted as success. He had a lovely wife and family, a beautiful home in Sussex and a successful law practice. He attended church from time to time but it had no impact on his life. At the age of 45 he found himself wondering whether or not God was real. Not wanting to ask other people, he decided to try and find out for himself, and went along to the public library to find books about people who had been born again. Finally convinced by what he read, one night he got on his knees in the sitting room and asked Jesus to come into his life.

Very soon after that, not having spoken to anyone about it, Peter was invited to an FGBMFI meeting. When the speaker had finished his testimony and asked if anyone wanted to publicly commit their lives to Jesus, Peter rushed to the front of the restaurant and for the first time experienced the Holy Spirit. Some months later, he received the baptism of the Holy Spirit, a powerful experience. For almost an hour, he could feel the incredible power pumping through his body. From his first meeting, Peter knew that he had to join the Fellowship, and that he would be in a position of leadership. He became a national director and secretary of the National Board, as well as being a local chapter president.

Peter has travelled to Kenya, Madrid, Warsaw and America for the Fellowship. The trip to Kenya had perhaps the greatest impact on him, when he was able to see, despite all the national problems, the tremendous enthusiasm of the FGBMFI men in that country. He has become a lay reader in the Church of England, because his spiritual life and growth through the FGBMFI have given him the desire to serve God in a greater way than ever before. Having, as he puts it, led a double life with the Church for 45 years, he has now been able to come, spiritually, to his full potential.

Although they are from a very different background, for Martin and Sue Sullivan going to an FGBMFI meeting proved to be an equally life-changing experience. They had both come from very difficult backgrounds, Sue had suffered all kinds of abuse and Martin had got into drugs and drink. Sue, a nurse, was coming to the point of giving up her chosen career because of severe rheumatoid arthritis, and the strains on the marriage were such that one Thursday evening they decided they could not go on any longer. The next evening, Friday, they would go their separate ways. However, that very evening Martin's brother rang and invited them, not for the first time, to an FGBMFI dinner in Retford, and Martin surprised everyone by agreeing to go on their last evening together.

The speaker at the dinner was Alan Pimlott from Norwich, a great singer and testifier. At the end of the evening, Alan invited anyone who wanted to see their lives changed by the power of Jesus to raise their hands as an indication that they wanted to ask Him into their lives. Unknown to each other, both Martin and Sue did this. Alan then asked the people who had responded to go forward to the front. Martin and Sue looked at each other in amazement and asked the other what they were doing as they stood and made their way to the front of the hotel room. Having prayed with Alan, they had both turned to come back to their seats when Sue heard him saying something about people wanting to be healed. Despite those already waiting, Sue turned round and pushed to stand in front of Alan again and said she wanted healing, indicating the huge lump she had at the base of her spine and her deformed hands, caused through the arthritis. As Alan prayed in the name of Jesus for her healing, the lump instantly disappeared, together with all the other symptoms of rheumatoid arthritis. Martin was also delivered that night, from drugs and drink.

There was no more talk of separation. Sue says it was as if the whole of their past life, from that moment, was gone and forgotten. Some time after this, Martin felt God calling him to Bible College, and he gave up his job and trained to become a minister. He and Sue were able not only to do a tremendous work for God in a town near Pontefract, but also to travel to Germany, America and, very dear to their heart, to Africa. Here they helped with a nursery and the church to which it belonged, and had the opportunity to travel and preach, with one or two hair-raising experiences thrown in for good measure.

Dave and Pam Drinnon were like many people in the UK. They had been to church most of their lives, but did not know you could have a personal relationship with Jesus. Good friends of theirs had been inviting them to a dinner in Hull over many months, and eventually they gave in. They were a bit late arriving and so did not, as they would normally, go to the bar for some wine. That night they heard a man pour out his heart with such feeling – telling things that were not easy to share. As always, people were asked to come forward for prayer at the end of the evening, but they didn't see any particular need to join in. However, their friend Helen asked them if they wanted to go, and at the second request they felt obligated.

While they had been watching people being prayed for, they had seen a number of them fall on the floor. Pam had never seen anyone overcome by the power of the Holy Spirit in this way and had it all worked out in her mind. Their daughter had been doing a psychology course, and they had discussed how people responded when they felt their personal space was being invaded. Pam decided that this was the reason for people falling, and there was no way she was going to do that. As the man prayed over her, Pam felt herself leaning backwards and tried to force herself upright, thinking to herself, 'I know what you're doing and it won't work on me!' The next thing she knew, she was lying on the very nice carpet next to her husband. Afterwards, Pam was so glad that she hadn't had a glass of wine that night, so there was no logical explanation for what had happened to her and David. Shortly afterwards, they both asked Jesus to come into their lives in a new way and to direct their future.

David's job then took him to America for three years, and it was there that they began to grow spiritually and came to realize exactly what that commitment had meant. During their time in the US, they were invited to participate in a training course to become counsellors for a Christian telephone helpline. Pam said that for her, during the first hour of training, the pieces of the jig-saw came together, and she knew that God was calling them into the work. Her immediate thought was, 'We are going to take this back to the UK.'

On their return to the UK, God enabled them to set up Cross Line, a Christian telephone helpline that aims to reach people at their point of need. God, they say, has changed their way of thinking and of praying. Because someone invited them to an FGBMFI dinner, two people were touched by the Holy Spirit, and an avenue of ministry opened up which otherwise may never have happened.

In London, a member of the Fellowship from America, Jerome Wagenius, was walking out one afternoon with his wife, doing some shopping. At one point the pavement ('sidewalk' in his words) dropped about four inches and, not noticing this, he stumbled and fell. He was carrying things in each hand, and so put his arm in front of his chest to try and cushion the fall. He hit the edge of the kerb with the centre of his arm and felt it break. People came out of the store to help him up. They wanted to call an ambulance as he was in terrible pain, but he refused; his wife was still inside the store and he needed to find her. When they got back to the house where they were staying, the host's wife, a nursing tutor, examined the arm and said she was sure it was broken. They all prayed, but Jerome got no relief from the pain. Deciding that there was no way he could go to a meeting and pray for healing for others if his own arm was in a plaster cast, he determined to go on and finish the series of meetings and trust the Lord to heal him.

That night, when he stood up to share his testimony the pain was so bad he had difficulty keeping his mind on what he was saying. Eventually, Jerome realized he was repeating himself, so he stopped and explained why he was experiencing problems, then pulled up his sleeve. When he gripped his hand tight, the people could see the bone bulge out at the side of his arm. Some people went and felt the separation of the bone. Not being able to carry on, Jerome told them he was going to cut the meeting short but asked first if there was anyone who wanted to come to know Jesus. Four people came up, and one of these was a man in a wheelchair. He said that he had broken his back two years before, just below his neck, and had been paralysed ever since. As soon as he had made a commitment to Jesus, this man asked for prayer for his back. Jerome lifted his broken arm in the air and squeezed the man's hand. The more he squeezed the less was the pain, until eventually he was able to hit his arm at the point of the break without any pain whatsoever. The man in the wheelchair said, 'Now I can believe.' Before he went home that night, he was able to lift himself up with his hands and move his hips round and round. After returning to America, Jerome received many letters telling of other, medically verified, healings.

Lincoln, one of the UK's great historical cities, had not had an active chapter for many years. Many men had prayed that it should restart, and no one more than John Wright, Director at Large for the Fellowship, formerly a national director and chapter president, based in Norwich. John had been in Loughborough for a national men's weekend and came out of the hotel into the car park to set off for home.

A man outside the hotel entrance was having problems with his car and, never one to miss an opportunity, John explained to him the way of salvation and told him he needed to be born again. The man – David – who just happened to live in Lincoln, told John that he was already a Christian. Nothing daunted, John then told him he should start a chapter of the FGBMFI in that city. With a little encouragement, that's exactly what David did, and Lincoln became a thriving chapter.

Another story about catching the vision concerns John Wright, a man who is well known throughout the Fellowship as a fearless witness to the power of salvation in whatever circumstance he happens to be. Driving out of a car park across a main road at 6.55 on a misty September morning, John saw the road was clear. Three seconds later, a Ford XR3, driven at considerable speed, crashed into his offside passenger door. Both cars were damaged beyond repair, but both drivers escaped with minor cuts and bruises. John describes that as a combination of the grace of God and the Volvo side impact support system!

Knowing that all things work together for good to those who love God and being a good Full Gospel Business Man, he had a pocketful of *Voice* magazines packed with testimonies of lives changed by God. These John gave out to the publican who gave him a cup of tea at the roadside, the policeman who took details, the ambulance man who took him to casualty for a check-up, the lady radiographer, the Hindu doctor and the nurses. Also, left alone in his cubicle for 45 minutes, he used the time to sing praises to God, albeit in a rather quivering voice!

Looking for a replacement grey Volvo estate on the Internet, John found one in Lincoln. He agreed a price with the salesman, Phil Birley, subject to the insurance company agreeing a write-off. Ten minutes later, Autosave, the company on the Internet, called from Sheffield. They knew of a similar car, with more mileage but £2,000 cheaper. He grabbed it, subject to the insurance company giving the go-ahead. Then he called Phil Birley to say that the deal was off as he had had a better offer. Phil accepted his decision without any fuss.

It was at that point that John was convicted by the Holy Spirit. 'Blessed is the man who keeps his word upon a contract even though it be to his own loss' (Psalm 15: 4). He called a friend to discuss it, and the friend confirmed what John already knew: he had to buy the more expensive car from Lincoln. He called Autosave and, providentially, they had not had time to buy the car. Then John called Phil Birley.

'My Father has been speaking to me,' John said. 'He told me I had to keep my word and have your car even though it is going to cost me £2,000 more.' John could tell that Phil was a little amazed at this divine intervention, but they arranged that he would drive the car to Nottingham station, where John would pick it up and Phil would then take the train back to Lincoln. As it happened, John got a lift to Nottingham. Five miles east of the city they stopped to get some petrol. John took the opportunity to go into the shop and buy a cup of hot chocolate, and as he walked out a thought came into his mind. 'There is your car.'

Four cars were being filled with petrol. The one in front of him was a grey Volvo estate. 'You are Phil Birley,' he said to the young man attending to it. He looked up in astonishment and said, 'Yes, but who are you?'

'Your customer!' John replied, with a smile.

'But that's incredible, incredible,' said Phil, overwhelmed by the impossibility and wonder of it all.

'Not at all', said John. 'Archbishop William Temple said, "When I pray coincidences happen and when I don't, they don't."'

John reflected on the odds against two cars meeting in this way. That they were both short of petrol at the same time was not too unusual. But to choose the same garage and arrive at the same moment, and then for John to recognize a car he wasn't expecting was astonishing. Almost, one might say, beyond belief!

Not the end of the story. Six weeks later, John was speaking at the Hull chapter and invited Phil, collecting him along the way. He was born again and baptized with the Holy Spirit at that dinner meeting.

As John frequently told the members of the Fellowship, being able to give a testimony to anyone, in any place, at any time, is what being a Christian and a good FGBMFI man is all about. He would quote Romans 15:18–19:

> For I will not dare to speak of any of those things which Christ has not accomplished through me, in word and deed, to make the Gentiles obedient – in mighty signs and wonders, by the power of the Spirit of God, so that from Jerusalem and round about to Illyricum I have fully preached the gospel of Christ.

Many of the chapters in the UK have regular visits in local prisons, an area which became a very important part of the Fellowship's work. A report to the Home Office on the Wolds Remand Prison made the following comments under the heading of 'Religious needs':

> Although attendance at formal religious services is generally low, prisoners appear to make good use of the less formal contacts with the Chaplaincy team, and of the volunteers who augment it ... Regular visits from outside singing groups are popular ... The dinners, hosted by the Full Gospel Business Men's Fellowship with the prisoners as

guests, were a great success. The catering, paid for by the Fellowship, was done by ARA staff and the meals were held in the staff facilities. We welcome such involvement by an outside group and hope that it will continue.[1]

These dinners took place because the chaplain of the Wolds Prison went along to an FGBMFI dinner and the following morning rang the president of the chapter. He said he liked what he had seen the previous evening, and could the chapter come into the prison and do the same thing? There would, however, be two small differences. One, the Fellowship would have to pay, and two, they could not take an offering! The members of the chapter and supporters at the dinners gave generously to enable this work to continue because they saw and heard what God was doing among the prisoners.

At one of the dinners, Johnny Hamilton, a man who radiated the love of Jesus, was sharing his testimony. When the meeting was over, Johnny put two chairs on one side and said he would sit in one and if anyone wanted to come and sit in the other and talk to him, he would pray with them. A man of about 60 staggered forward on crutches, and very soon both he and Johnny had tears running down their faces. Forty years previously, the man had been a member of a Pentecostal church and was engaged to a young lady from the same church. Sadly, she died and he had become so bitter and angry that he had turned his back on God. That night in the Wolds, he recommitted his life to Jesus, and the following Sunday stood up in the prison chapel and told how his life had been turned around.

SEVEN

Impact on Europe

The men in the United States who had caught the vision of the Fellowship looked towards Europe as a strategic area, perhaps because so many had their roots in that part of the world. Tommy Hicks and other leading evangelists were vitally important in helping the work overseas. Russia, Switzerland, Ireland, Finland and West Germany saw meetings of business men held and chapters formed. Then in 1961, the first European convention took place in Zurich, Switzerland, in the great Kongresshaus, where 18 nations were represented.

Howard Anderson from Connecticut left teaching to become an ordained minister. The image that might conjure up is far from reality. His first 'mission field' was Alaska, where he went round villages, a sleeping bag under one arm, a banjo in the other hand, and a small Bible in his pocket. He would knock on the first Eskimo door in a village and ask if there was anyone sick. Remarkable healings took place as Anderson fulfilled Luke 10:8–9, 'Whatever city you enter, and they receive you ... heal the sick there, and say to them, "The kingdom of God has come near to you".' He subsequently travelled the world, preaching in campaigns and FGBMFI chapter meetings, but he kept remembering the first FGBMFI breakfast he attended, when Oral Roberts spoke. Going home afterwards, Anderson had fallen on his knees, and God had spoken to him, telling him to go to Scandinavia. In April of 1960, five years later, he was obedient to that call. When he heard that the Fellowship were holding the World Convention in London in 1965, he made contact with them and arranged for Simon Vikse, the president of the New York chapter, to bring a team over to Sweden. Anderson also influenced a Swedish business man, R. Pellen, to publish the first *Voice* magazine in Swedish in that year. A photograph in *Airlift to London*, the publication that reported the airlift, shows Demos in his large Stetson, face beaming, receiving a copy of that particular *Voice*.

The team that visited Sweden was only one of many organized to travel throughout Europe during the week following the convention. In Gothenburg, the first meeting was arranged for after Sunday evening services. A Christian youth centre was booked and refreshments provided. Expecting around 300, a larger crowd than usual, they were amazed to find the halls, the foyer and the entrance stairway all crowded, the room itself packed, and young people standing everywhere. Around 80 people responded for prayer, some accepting Jesus for the first time, and many of them receiving the baptism of the Holy Spirit.

Other successful meetings were held throughout the week, by the end of which two other teams joined them on their way back to London, one having visited Norway and the other Finland. Representatives from Norway and Finland also came over, so that it was truly a meeting of all Scandinavia. One of the Americans, of Swedish descent, wrote:

The thing that stirred my heart during this Spiritual Airlift that reached so many countries and denominations, was that so many of these business men, coming together from varied theological backgrounds, were so filled with the Spirit of God and so enjoying the fellowship that none wanted to bring up any theological debate that would hinder or divide. In my heart, I had felt that many denominations could never come together; but a miracle took place there. God is using the Full Gospel Business Men to bring this thing to pass – to fill the gap that must be filled. They are stirring up laymen to go forth as personal witnesses.

One thing we need to know is that when we move under the anointing of the Holy Spirit, the Holy Spirit does not compete against Himself. As pastors, evangelists, and business men, we need to understand that God has put us in our particular place, not to compete against one another, but to complement one another. How wonderfully the spirit of FGBMFI bridges that gap.[1]

One couple on the Swedish team came from Portland, Oregon. They set their suitcases down on the street in the Swedish town to which they had been assigned, unsure of precisely where they were supposed to go. A young man was walking along the street, so they stopped him, and to their relief he spoke English. He helped them make a telephone call, and as he was about to leave the lady took a Gospel tract from her bag and handed it to him. It had the address of their local church on it. As the young man turned the tract over, he suddenly shouted out, 'You're from Portland! Don't you remember me? I was in your church, with another man, two months ago.' By then the couple had recalled the occasion when this young man had decided to become a Christian. His friend however, had refused. The young man went on to tell them that as they were boarding their ship the next day, his companion missed the gangplank and drowned in the Willamette river.

As a result of the airlift, successful meetings were also held in Norway and Finland. In the late 1990s, a new move of the Spirit of God seems to have touched these countries again. In 1999, seven members from Norway spent five days in Torshavn, Faroe Islands. The men felt they were in the right place at the right time. All the people they met were enthusiastic; a chapter has started, and they expect it to grow and have an impact on the islands. As was so often the case with countries that have themselves been blessed by airlifts, their own men began to reach out in similar ways to spread the vision.

In Berlin, Germany, the men assigned to that country from the airlift joined forces with T.L. Osborne and a great campaign was held where many were saved, healed and filled with the Holy Spirit. An American naval base at Rota, some 125 miles north of the Rock of Gibraltar, was the venue for yet another group. Here the invitation came through the wife of a naval officer whom members of the group had known in Portland. This lady was very active and something of a leader in the social and spiritual clubs on the base. Because of this, she was able to arrange a dinner to which a group of officers were invited, as well as meetings in the chapel, the prison and places outside the base.

When God has used people in such wonderful ways, it doesn't mean that everything else will be plain sailing. This group visiting Gibraltar set off for the airport in what they thought was good time, but they had not allowed for the border gates. They arrived ten minutes after the Spanish guard had closed the gates for the night. Nothing could persuade him to open them again until *mañana* (tomorrow). They stood there and watched their plane take off, knowing there would not be another until the following Thursday, too late for them to catch their plane to the United States. All efforts having failed at that point, they drove to the city of Malaga, about 100 miles along the Mediterranean coast. There they were able to turn in their airline tickets to obtain passage from Malaga to London, but would not arrive until three hours after their SAS plane to America had left. They prayed and read from 2 Chronicles chapter 20, in which God states, 'the battle is not yours but mine and I will make a way where there is no way'. To their amazement, the flights manager of Scandinavian Air Services called to advise them that their 12 o'clock flight had been cancelled, but the airline were willing to purchase a ticket for them on Pan American Airlines and bill them later in America. Within 40 minutes, they had their tickets and were aboard a Pan Am plane for Los Angeles.

France provided a more unusual venue when on three days members of the team visited a gypsy camp near Paris. This was some experience, when the Spirit of God was felt in the most marvellous way, especially through the singing. The church had only a few benches and was packed with people sitting on the concrete floor, which was covered with lovely throw-over rugs. Patience was needed as the preacher spoke in Spanish, was interpreted into French, and was then interpreted into English. It didn't seem to matter. The people were thoroughly blessed and keen for the men to go back again.

In the Netherlands, a minister whose origins were rooted in that area led the group. They too saw many people born again, healed and filled with the Holy Spirit. A restaurant manager said to him, 'I want you to know, sir, that these men have challenged my soul. I never knew that there was a group of people who could manifest such a wonderful spirit towards each other and also towards the world around them.'

One of the biggest teams, 37 in all, went to Rome, Italy. The Catholic bishop from one of the eastern states in the

USA told what God had meant to him since he had been filled with the Holy Spirit. A report on one of the services tells of a high-ranking Communist official who, receiving a handbill advertising the meeting, angrily stamped it into the ground. However, he was persuaded by the young people of that church to attend. He made sure he sat as far back as possible, but that didn't stop the Spirit of God from reaching out to him, and he committed his life to Jesus Christ in that meeting. The following night he brought two former comrades, who also became Christians, and on the third evening he brought his wife, son and daughter-in-law. All three were born again. In those same meetings, an old lady, badly crippled for some time as the result of a car accident, was wonderfully healed after receiving prayer.

Team member Tony Salerno was able to take a group back to his home town of Bagheria in Sicily. Tony still had many of his family there, and when the plane landed in Palermo the group was quickly surrounded by a number of very excitable Italians, all talking at once and all making them most welcome. They were able to spend a week talking to the family and friends, and they had the privilege of seeing 28 of them accept the Lord as their Saviour. Tony's nephew, who had been carrying such a weight of hatred in his heart that he had been unable to accept Jesus, found that the Holy Spirit was able to turn that hatred to love. His 92-year-old aunt said that since receiving Jesus into her heart she felt like a new person, so full of peace that even her body felt stronger!

In all of the countries to which teams went out from London in 1965, the work of the Fellowship remained ongoing, and it enabled a much stronger base to be established from which the FGBMFI was able to grow and extend throughout most of the countries of Europe and beyond.

In 1966 a European Convention was held in Switzerland. Demos and his wife Rose were present in Zurich, along with about a hundred FGBMFI men and women from the United States, as well as men and women from all over Europe. About half of the Americans had travelled on from the World Pentecostal Conference in Jerusalem, Israel. As with almost all of these meetings and conventions, there were outstanding instances of salvation, healing and receiving of the Holy Spirit. The Zurich chapter held a special luncheon for the leaders and men of the Fellowship, including those from the International of the FGBMFI and from chapters in Europe and as far away as Hong Kong.

Miner Arganbright and Thomas Nickel had visited Europe in 1957, assisting in establishing chapters of the FGBMFI in Ireland, Germany, Switzerland and Greece. This visit, along with the 1965 London airlift, made the European Convention possible. In appreciation of their work, both men were given token gifts and honoured publicly by the leaders in Europe.

Perhaps taking the idea from London, the organizers arranged for two weeks of meetings for some of the men after the convention. They visited Heilbronn, Hanover and Karlsruhe in Germany, and Utrecht and The Hague in Holland. Demos, Rose and Thomas Nickel attended all of these. One pastor from Holland said, 'What occurred at the convention, and what has happened at these meetings since, has accomplished more for the evangelization of Europe than all of our combined efforts for the past twenty years!' Another pastor declared, 'Nothing, neither organizations nor individuals, no force, can stop this move of God in Europe now, or ever!'

Two years later, Simon Vikse of Long Island, New York, Henry Carlson of Chicago and Enoch Christofferson of Turlock, California, all three men of Scandinavian descent, 'took up the cause of the airlift, and developed it into a major evangelistic tool'.[2] Over the years, Vikse and Carlson, founders of the Chicago chapter, organized several airlifts to Scandinavian countries. They were described as 'FGBMFI apostles to northern Europe', while Christofferson turned his attention to the Far East.

EIGHT

Ever-widening Ripples

Steve Lightle, a Jew, was a man who had travelled extensively for the Fellowship throughout the UK and Europe since 1976. He became a Christian while a student at university, but had never heard of the power of the Holy Spirit being in the life of a believer – that is, not until August of 1970. One Saturday morning he attended a breakfast meeting of the Seattle chapter, and was so impressed by what he heard that he went to a luncheon meeting the following Wednesday, where he was baptized in the Holy Spirit. From that day on, he became very involved in the local chapter, and in April 1973 was one of a group of ten men who went on an airlift to Braunschweig in northern Germany. John Andor, a member of the Seattle chapter, had moved to Germany a few months earlier because of his job, and he asked them to organize the trip.

The night before the men were due to fly back to the United States, they were at a small prayer meeting in Braunschweig when there was a prophetic message that one of the Americans would come, with his family, and live in Braunschweig. At first, they joked a little among themselves, trying to work out who the person was. As they were going to the airport, tears came into Steve's eyes and be began to cry; much as he tried to control it, he could not. It was a cry that came from the bottom of his heart. He tried to talk about it with his friend from Seattle, Fred Doerflein, on the way home but every time their conversation began, Steve just sobbed and could not understand why.

God had been speaking to Steve over the preceding year as he began to sense that there were things coming into his life far more important than running a car wash. Anyone who knows Steve will smile at the title of the firm: Dippy Duck Car Wash. He is a man who has a tremendous sense of fun as well as a tremendous sense of destiny. One day, a few months before the German trip, the Lord spoke clearly to him, 'My son, the day will come when you will get up, leave this office and never return.' Steve was married with a family and all the financial commitments that ensue from that state. Having put all their savings into the car wash, it is not surprising that he found God's word to him difficult to believe. However, God was speaking to his wife Judy at the same time, and the Lord began to prepare them in small ways for the enormous changes that were to come.

In the February before Braunschweig, as Steve was putting all the business papers in order one night, the Lord spoke again to him, 'My son, today is the day. Get up, walk out of the office, and never return!' Steve knew that this was right, and there was no sense of fear. He got up and walked over to the safe to take out the money, about $14,000, and the cheque book. 'My son, that does not belong to you! It is not yours any more!' Steve's immediate and natural thought was to wonder how they were going to keep going; then it dawned on him that he was no longer the steward of the business. It was the beginning of a new life.

That night he could not find any peace in his heart, worrying about who would open the business the next morning, who would pay the staff, and so on. Before he went to bed, the phone rang. The man at the other end of the line told Steve that God had just spoken to him. He found it difficult to say the next bit – that God had told him to take over the car wash business – and was even more amazed when Steve was clearly over the moon about it. They arranged for him to pick up the keys, the combination to the safe and everything relevant to the business the following morning at six o'clock.

When, therefore, Steve returned from Braunschweig and told Judy all that had transpired, they began to fast and pray. Within six weeks, they and their two children flew back to live in Braunschweig, the last town on earth in which Steve, as a Jew, would naturally settle. Braunschweig is the town that gave Adolf Hitler his German citizenship; during the airlift to Germany, God had had to deal with Steve on his feelings concerning Germany and the Jews.

Just before he and his family left the United States for Braunschweig, Steve met a Jewish lady from Austria with the concentration camp tattoo on her arm. She came up to Steve and spat in his face, asking him how he could be such a traitor as to go to that city. Sadly, she did not understand how God could have filled his heart with such love for the people of that city and country.

The obvious place to start was in Braunschweig itself, where Steve, with John Andor, set up a chapter. It was slow and difficult in the beginning, but gradually the work began to spread as God began to move in the chapter meetings. Later that year, the two men organized a conference in the town, to which Demos and George Otis were invited as speakers. It was a considerable step of faith, but about 300 people came, from the surrounding countries as well as Germany. This was when the International decided to set up the European Office of the Fellowship. John Andor was asked to head up the office, and he gave up his job and moved his family to Brussels to undertake the task.

Steve travelled tirelessly throughout Europe and the UK, being a fantastic inspiration to the men. He also made them feel very uncomfortable at times, particularly the British. On one occasion, when they were setting up the chapters with Bob Spilman, they went to a restaurant and naturally said grace. But it was not a very 'British' grace. All holding hands, they sang without the slightest embarrassment – at least, the Americans did!

Eastern Europe also became a target for the European FGBMFI men. Steve had been working with two groups, the East European Bible Mission and Open Doors. In January 1976 he was arrested in East Germany and given his own private escort to the border, had his picture taken, then was literally thrown into West Berlin. That picture turned up in three nations, East Germany, Czechoslovakia and Hungary. Open Doors had arranged to give Steve a car to enable him to travel more easily; when he went to collect it, they said they could not use him any more because of his picture being circulated, but they were still prepared to give him the car.

Shortly after that, a European Convention was held in Brussels, largely organized by John Andor, and Steve was very despondent, feeling he had let so many people down. The Lord spoke to him and said, 'Can you go to the back of the room and just sit there?' He wondered if he could be faithful in that small thing. Wanting to go home, nevertheless he took note of the word from the Lord and stayed, sitting for four days in the back row. When everyone was leaving the hotel on Sunday morning, Steve went to the car park, but somehow went through the wrong door and came out at the front of the hotel, where he saw Demos Shakarian and Tommy Ashcraft.

'You are 90 seconds late,' said Demos. Steve's response was, 'Late for what?'

Demos said they were waiting for him because they wanted to talk to him about being the Director for Europe. John Andor was leaving Brussels and going back to America, and they wanted Steve to take over. He responded, 'You don't understand. God has finished with me and I'm going home.' The thing was, even though he was so despondent and genuinely thought things were over, Steve knew in his heart that God had told him in 1973 that he would be the Director for Europe. However, it was still a shock to him. He asked Demos to give him a week to fast and pray, and then he would give his answer.

Judy and he fasted and prayed, and the Lord said, 'You do it, but take no salary and no expenses. You will let them provide you with a car but, for the rest of it, look to Me for all the finances.'

When Demos received Steve's call and heard what God had said, he replied, 'I always pay people, but at the moment we have no finances and cannot pay you.' Steve told him he would need a car and it was provided, by the Seattle chapter. This chapter probably did more for the expansion of the FGBMFI throughout the world than almost any other. From the earliest days of the Fellowship, collectively it gave generously of its men and finances, and continues to do so.

Steve made an interesting observation regarding the way in which the Fellowship worked. God never told Demos to organize chapters, he says, but gave him a vision to call men back to Himself. Demos said the only way he knew how to do it was through chapters, 'but the anointing is on the vision, not the organization'.

Just to read the account of Steve's itineraries in the following four years makes one feel exhausted. Every spring and autumn, Demos and Rose came for a month, and they would go round all the conferences. He worked hard to set up the core organization in the UK and Ireland, and looked to the

Lord as to where he should go next: that turned out to be France. Again, he followed the same pattern, establishing the core leaders and ensuring they had fully grasped the vision and then letting them go and do it. Chapters were quickly formed all over France.

In Denmark, with Johannus Mulleig, in Switzerland with Johannus' brother, Gunnar, the same pattern was followed again. Then to Finland and Sweden, where Gunnar Olsson was appointed as the Director. Then to Norway, working with Sophus Schanke and Kora Nordley, the man who head-ed up Coca-Cola in Norway. Steve even brought Demos over to help make them understand the validity of FGBMFI. Once they had grasped it, they set to work, opening up chapters in the various countries and islands of Scandinavia. Austria was also targeted. Steve had met a pastor from Salzburg in 1973, and it was through him that they were able to meet up with people around Vienna, Spital and Graz. He saw his role as spending time with the men, finding people, sharing the vision and firing them up to do the job.

For four years, Steve and his family gave themselves whole-heartedly to the work of FGBMFI in Europe, but God had put another calling on his life: that of assisting Jews to get out of the then Soviet Union and to Israel. While in Braunschweig, he had received a vision from God and he knew this was to become his life-long work. The incredible story of this work can be read in two books by Steve Lightle, *Exodus II – Let My People Go* and *Operation Exodus II*.

In the summer of 1979, Steve went back to America, to Los Angeles, and told Demos that God wanted him to move to Israel. Demos said that before he left, he wanted him to give notice – three years' notice! Steve could not believe it. 'Demos, I love you and I respect you as my elder in the Lord, but ...' However, because of the love and respect he had for Demos, and the fact that in the past Steve had always checked everything out with him, he gritted his teeth and Demos got his three years. How understandable it was that Demos was reluctant to let Steve go. What a man! What an inspiration! His last official convention was the European at Wembley in 1980, and that was a tremendous blessing. So it was in late 1981 that Steve resigned and took his family to Israel to start his work on the second exodus.

The Fellowship, however, was greater than any individual. It was the power of the Holy Spirit, working out God's vision for it and bringing men and women into a full salvation. Nevertheless, from time to time there were particular men that God raised up to use in extraordinary ways. Dr Fred Ladenius was such a man. Born in the Netherlands, a brilliant linguist – he spoke eight languages fluently – Fred became press secretary to the much-loved pope, John XXIII. That was until he met Demos. As leader of the Catholic Charismatic Renewal in Italy, Fred encountered Demos in 1973 and the following year was invited to be one of the major speakers at the World Convention, along with Kenneth Hagin and Father John Bertolucci. That same year, Demos invited him to go to Brussels when the new European Headquarters opened, and asked him to start *Voice* magazine in different European editions. In Fred's words, it was then 'time for prayer'. God certainly knew his man when he chose Demos Shakarian to start this Fellowship, because Fred quickly accepted and spent the next seven years in Brussels.

Fred had the vision for starting chapters, and because of his gift for languages and the fact that he is a wonderfully erudite and amusing speaker, was much in demand all over the world. He was the first speaker at a banquet in Guatemala and went to Argentina, Brazil and Costa Rica, to name but a few countries in Latin America. One of the things that so attracted Dr Fred to the FGBMFI was that it encompassed people from all the Christian denominations; besides this, it reached business men, and he saw the importance and influence of women in the Fellowship, epitomized by Demos' wife, Rose.

During his time in Europe, the publication of *Voice* magazine grew, as he very successfully managed to combine editing this with an enormous amount of travelling and speaking. He is particularly remembered in Ireland for the time he first spoke there, something of a turning point in that country. A dinner was held in Dublin, and was significant for the fact that on the platform were Protestants from the north and Catholics from the south. In fact, it was the men from the north who had regularly travelled to the south to encourage and help set up chapters, something for which many of them paid a great price financially. Hector, the first Director in the north, had his shop set on fire on more than one occasion because he associated with Catholics. Praise God, this did not deter them in any way!

At this special dinner in Dublin was a man for whom this was all very new. Joe Dalton, a very popular amateur opera singer in Ireland for many years, had recently experienced the power of the Holy Spirit in his life. Joe had been in depression for 31 years. Despite the fact that he had a wife and family, a good job and was much in demand on the concert stage and radio, Joe could not find any relief from his depression. At that time he was a general manager for the Post Office Telephone Company in Dublin, and would travel every day on the train from Dun Laoghaire to the capital. He often noticed a man sitting in the same carriage, in Joe's words, 'with fuzzy hair and a silly grin'. For some reason he irritated Joe. This man was always reading what Joe described as 'holy books', Christian paperbacks. One day, when he could stand his silly grin no longer, Joe asked what it was he was reading. When the man told him it was about the Charismatic Renewal, Joe said he had no time for such rubbish and could not understand why he bothered. Then the man said something which to someone like Joe was very dangerous: 'Then why am I so happy, and why are you so miserable?' All his life Joe had had a very violent temper, once knocking out five men in a football match! As he often now says, the guy didn't know how dangerously he was living!

They went on to talk about less contentious issues, family and work, and to his amazement, Joe discovered that this man worked in the same building, was married with a family, had a mortgage, and in so many ways was like Joe, except he didn't sing. He offered Joe a book by Merlin Carothers, *From Prison To Praise*, and Joe said he would think about reading it.

One night, when Joe had finished reading the book and all the family were in bed, he got down on his knees and prayed. Now Joe was a devout Catholic and had faithfully attended mass all his life. He had renewed the vows made for him at baptism when he took his first communion. There was no doubt in his mind that God had sent Jesus to die for his sins. The problem was, he could find no release from the condemnation he felt – not, that is, until he read this book. 'God,' he said, 'if there is such a power as this man talks about, I want to receive it.' The room was in total darkness, it was very late and the curtains were drawn. Suddenly brilliant light filled the room and enveloped Joe, and he felt himself as it were cradled in the love of God. In an instant, his depression left him, never to return, and he found himself speaking in tongues. He had never heard anyone else speak in tongues, and as far as he knew, no one else in Ireland did!

Shortly after this experience he was invited to the FGBMFI dinner in Dublin and found himself sitting up at the front alongside Billy Burke, from the north, and Dr Fred Ladenius, having been asked to give a short testimony. After Joe had finished speaking, Fred stood up and said he had several words of knowledge (when God shows an individual things about a situation or about people). He turned to Joe and said, 'God has given you a healing ministry.' Joe had no idea what he meant. He often says he couldn't even 'heel a pair of shoes', let alone a person! But God knew what He was doing. Invitations began to come from all over Ireland for Joe to speak and share his testimony, and eventually he felt compelled to give up his full-time employment and devote his whole life to serving God in this new way. Immediately, the invitations to sing dried up; until then, Joe had been out almost every night of the week at some engagement or other. Now God had something new for him.

Joe joined the FGBMFI and started to travel, not just around Ireland, but eventually to the UK, Malta, Yugoslavia, Italy, America and many other places. He has spoken to hundreds of thousands of people all over the world, and has seen God move mightily in salvation, healing and baptism in the Holy Spirit.

After Dr Fred Ladenius had given seven years to overseeing *Voice* in Europe, he moved to Switzerland, where he continued to be involved with the chapters there and also with a Christian TV programme that went out in Italy. He carried on speaking for the Fellowship, and when he talked about Demos Shakarian he did so with tremendous love and affection. He was, to Fred, 'the most wonderful man I have ever met'.

A new man was needed to take over the job of editing and publishing *Voice*, and this time it was Canadian-born Blair Scott, whose father had been very involved in the Fellowship, both in America and then on the west coast of Canada. He and his wife had good jobs and were prosperous, but felt they had to do something to help extend the Kingdom of God. Having gone to Bible School and then trained for participating in the Christian outreach at the Moscow Olympics, Blair felt compelled one day to ring his father and tell him that he didn't know why he was phoning, except God had told him to. His father said, 'I will phone you back in two days.' As promised, his father rang back and told Blair he had wanted to check something out. Steve Lightle had been to see him two weeks before Blair phoned, to say that he had had a vision from God and saw Blair working in the European Office of FGBMFI. 'Would you be open to this?' asked his dad. Blair and his wife Gayle wanted more than anything to go back home, but they decided that if you were to call Jesus 'Lord', then you did whatever He asked. God gave them the grace and the means to stay in Europe for many years, work-ing with *Voice* magazine, and they did not go back to the United States until 1999. Modern technologies no longer require people to be in specific places any more!

Although there were some extraordinary men, in people's eyes, God saw them as ordinary men, men who were not only willing but were also obedient to do His will. There were, and have been over the years, thousands and thousands of 'ordinary' members of the Fellowship whom God used. They didn't always hit the headlines, but without them, the FGBMFI could not have grown, or continue to grow, in the miraculous way it did.

NINE

The Golden Chain

The late 1970s and 1980s saw dramatic growth across Europe. In Germany, Dr Ulrich von Schnurbein and his wife, Barbara, had become Christians at university, and when they returned to their small mountain village found they missed the close fellowship and comradeship they had experienced with other students. Through various contacts, they began to understand their need for the baptism of the Holy Spirit to better equip them to fulfil the calling they believed God had placed on their lives. They began travelling to Munich to share in fellowship they felt was lacking at home, and here they heard for the first time about the FGBMFI. In 1979, they started the Deggendorf chapter, and through those dinner meetings they came into contact with Mennonites, Baptists, Charismatic Catholics and others. In their words, 'Our borders were being expanded and we saw the need for unity amongst Christians of all denominations.'[1] Ulrich and his family lived in the Bavarian Forest, where they ran a logging company and a holiday resort. He became an International Director and President of the work in Germany, and travelled throughout Europe, particularly in the former Yugoslavia.

In Austria, a man called Winfried Fuchs became the highest-paid business management seminar speaker in the German-speaking world, but at a price! Very much into New Age and positive thinking, he committed so much of his time and energy to pursuing his business goals that his marriage broke up. Eventually he married again, but despite his best intentions the second marriage degenerated to the same depths as the first. Professionally, everything was great, but his personal life was in crisis and his health began to suffer. Winfried began having blackouts to the extent that he could no longer continue in his profession.

At this point of crisis, he made contact with another management consultant who, on seeing the condition he was in, told him, 'Only Jesus can help you!' This man suggested he go to a large conference called Berlin 81, and this was where Winfried and his wife Maria committed their lives to Jesus. They were then invited to a seminar led by the Charismatic Renewal, when they both received the baptism of the Holy Spirit. In their marriage was a new joy and peace.

The management consultant who first shared with him was a member of the FGBMFI and it was through him that Winfried became involved. He now has the privilege of standing before business men and managers, sharing management techniques which are not based on man's ideas but on biblical principles. Winfried worked throughout Austria, opening chapters, and in 1990 organized the All European convention in Innsbruck. For the last ten years of the millennium, Winfried had a vision for what he called 'God's Managers', people who would rise up in the businessplace and practice biblical principles in management as well as in their private lives. Seeing an army of God's Managers was the main theme of a convention in Austria. Following the conference, Richard Shakarian and Blair Scott shared at the FGBMFI chapter in Salzburg, where the local men put on a first-class showpiece evening. Even though the press and TV news media were present, the power of the living God shone through. Of course, a large number of the many visitors wanted to enter into the kind of relationship with Christ they spoke of. It was exciting and alive!

> Airlifts have played an important part in the FGBMFI over the years. There is something about going to another nation that lifts a man's faith and helps him to reach beyond himself to witness and pray with people. Once he sees the miracles take place, there is a double benefit. The nation is built up for ongoing work, and his faith is ignited. When he returns home, that man or woman often has renewed fire and vision, which in turn impacts the local work. I think back at the blessing our first airlifts were, from Seattle, Washington, to our sister city, Nantes, in France. That was such a blessing that it started a series of outreaches that are still going on today.[2]

It was during the Brussels convention in May 1976 that Frenchmen present first began to plan for a chapter in Paris. They would ultimately conduct their own convention, similar to the one held in Brussels, but this idea was really born in the July 1976 world convention in Miami, Florida. They wasted no time and held that first French convention in September the following year. The following excerpt was taken from the newspaper *Ouest-France*. Under the headline 'Businessmen About the Business of God: A Spirituality Come from Abroad', part of the report reads:

> The waiters of the *Concorde-Lafayette*, the Parisian palace of Porte-Mayot, had never seen that; neither had France: the businessmen they had been serving for three days invited them, at the end of a 500-place closing dinner, to mount the

podium in order to applaud and pray for them. A wonderful singing in tongues, prayer of praise to God, swelled up and visibly impressed the waiters, little accustomed to such honours. The businessmen coming from America to the first Full Gospel Business Men's French convention, held these last few days in Paris, set the tone for the newborn French community. And 240,000 Americans of FGBMFI, or 10,000 an hour, were praying at the same moment for a revival in France.

'His banner over us is love.' The Bible verse from the Song of Solomon could be read in giant letters above the podium where God's witnesses came, one after another to tell their stories. There is a long list of those who can tell, like the little Jewess of Nazareth, of the 'wonders of the Lord' done in their lives. Like the well-known surgeon from Oklahoma, receiving professional honours in his field, but 'miserable', an alcoholic, drugged to the limit, condemned by other doctors, 'miraculously healed' and converted, after 43 years without God.

'You know, businessmen are hard. But when Jesus touches their hearts, they soften up!' says Demos Shakarian, founder of the International Fellowship, to those who will have as their task, in the months to come, the establishment of a hundred or so chapters of FGBMFI in France.[3]

Another major event hosted by France took place in Grenoble in 1987. Bruno Berthon, the International Director for France, was encouraged by the united effort of the French members in organizing the European convention, which took place that summer. The first hall they looked at held only fifteen hundred people, and they believed it would be too small. Their faith was well rewarded, as there were over 5,500 in most of the evening meetings, the highest attendance being around 7,000.

Probably the most outstanding meeting took place on the Thursday afternoon, when Reinhard Bonnke was the speaker. At the end of his powerful message, hundreds of people came forward for prayer and healing. At least ten people received healing of impaired hearing and five witnessed to being healed of partial blindness, many others also being touched by God. Of the miracles that happened, the most dramatic was that of Yvon Vendevill, from Nantes in France. Only two months before the convention, neurological tests had revealed a benign tumour compressing his spinal cord just where the nerves branch out to the lower limbs. Four weeks before the convention, an operation was carried out and the family fully expected they would not be able to travel to Grenoble.

The day before Yvon entered hospital, the family came together to pray and listen to a cassette of worship songs. When they formed a circle and prayed for Yvon, he felt shivers shooting through his whole body. Removing the meningioma was a very long and delicate operation, and he spent one day in an intensive care unit, then six days totally immobilized. God gave him a great sense of peace and, through a vision, Yvon learned that this trial would strengthen his faith. He needed that assurance because post-operative complications developed: hypersensitivity in his right arm, weakness in his left side, and problems with his neck. Still, after ten days he was allowed to leave hospital. A brace was attached, and each day he had to spend an hour with the physiotherapist, learning to walk again. His left hand no longer had any strength in it. Miraculously, he was able to travel by air to Grenoble, but had to use a wheelchair.

At the beginning of his message that afternoon, Bonnke stopped, pointed down to Yvon and said that God had shown him, before he had come to the meeting, that there would be a man in a wheelchair who would be healed. 'That man,' said

Bonnke, 'was you.' He asked Yvon to come up to the front of the stadium, where Bonnke prayed for him and told him to stand up in the name of Jesus. After a moment's hesitation, Yvon did so, and felt the strength come back into his legs. As the convention was being held in the Sport Palace, there was a first-aid room so, with a physiotherapist and his wife, Yvon went down to the room, where they checked him out and removed the neck brace. When he came back in the evening, two French doctors examined him and confirmed that he could hold his head normally and that he had been healed!

Returning home from Grenoble, he visited two doctors. The first one was not a Christian and had no explanation for the recovery. The second was a Christian and understood that God had performed a miracle of healing. X-rays confirmed the miracle.

An even bigger event than Grenoble was held in 1997 in the Palais Omnisports de Paris Bercy, the biggest indoor conference centre in the country. Visitors came from all over Europe, Africa, the Caribbean and North America, with at least 10,000 people in some of the meetings. Worship was the main emphasis, and thousands joined their voices together, lifting up the name of Jesus. Even unbelievers were caught up in the spirit of worship. It was not possible to enter into such a tangible sense of the present of the living God and be unmoved. At the end of the opening session, more than a thousand people came forward to receive Jesus Christ into their lives. Jesus said that if we would lift Him up, He would draw all men unto Himself. This is what took place in Bercy.

Something different in that convention was when Olympic athletes shared an unforgettable 'Evening with the Stars' hosted by Sam Mings from Lay Witnesses for Christ. Each member of the delegation was a champion in their discipline and simply witnessed to the power of the God they served. They electrified the people with their stories and challenged everyone to fulfil God's plan for their lives. Once again, the front of the stadium was flooded with people responding to an invitation to accept Jesus as their Lord and Saviour.

The following year, a weekend was held specifically for leaders in the Fellowship. Lynn Heritage, an FGBMFI area representative from south-east Wales, was one of those present. As soon as *Voice* magazine arrived, giving details of the weekend, he felt compelled to attend, and within an hour of receiving the magazine had booked the convention and the flight. On the outward journey he discovered that the people sitting next to him were also going – John Mason (vice president of the Milton Keynes chapter) and his wife, Maureen. What struck Lynn more than anything about this weekend was a key message by John Carrette. He summed up how Demos saw the work of the FGBMFI[4] as five simple steps to making a chapter member:

1 to get the person saved;
2 to get the person delivered;
3 to get the person healed;
4 to introduce them to the anointing of the Holy Spirit;
5 to send them out to do likewise.

When he heard these words, Lynn realized the purpose of his visit to France. In his words:

> It was to improve the quality of my conversations and to improve the understanding of chapter members. The FGBMFI is a wonderful vehicle to serve the Lord, but individual members should search their hearts for the Lord's purpose in their lives ... If they are called to reach people through Full Gospel Business Men's Fellowship International, then they should be single-minded in their efforts, in order to reap an abundant harvest.[5]

In being obedient to God's word, the directors and members of France enabled many members, Christians and non-Christians, to see, hear and experience the power of God in the lives of men and women. It was described in *Networking*, the interactive news report of the Fellowship, as 'a new wave of the Spirit within FGBMFI', a new move of the Holy Spirit among many of the nations in Europe.

Donato Anzalone and Michael Kayembe toured the Belgian chapters in the late 1990s, and everyone felt that the meetings helped revive the vision for starting new chapters. Since then, several new chapters have been formed. The Belgian national president, Raoul Richez, said, 'God has shown FGBMFI lately that all chapters will not be the same, "each chapter will be an expression of God's infinite variety". In this vein two youth chapters are being formed.'[6] This was followed up later in the year with a national convention at which a tremendous sense of excitement was experienced. One young woman, 21 years old, with acute leukaemia, was declared by doctors to be totally healed after she had received prayer in the name of Jesus. A man who had for many years suffered from arthritis walked away, leaving his cane and wheelchair behind after being prayed for. Another person was healed from a problem with the thyroid gland. People were set free from terrible depressions, and demons had to flee in the name of Jesus. In his report of this convention, Rik Van Neste described it as a fresh outpouring of the Holy Spirit, bringing a new sense of unity for the work of the FGBMFI. 'There was a realization that this convention was just a glimpse of what Jesus wants to do through believers in these last days. As Jesus put it, "The harvest is great and the labourers are few..." Therefore pray with us in expectation for more of these kinds of happenings, and that God would pour out His spirit in an even greater measure.'[7]

In Switzerland at around the same time, God encouraged the men to focus on fellowship.

In order to become a team, FGBMFI members need time with one another. Love will grow out of this and will touch those who do not yet know Jesus Christ in a personal way. With this in mind, Swiss members are spending more time getting to know each other. The result in one chapter was that out of the 60 people attending their outreach meeting, half were there for the first time and 18 made a commitment to Jesus Christ.[8]

In Finland, they had a word from God for their nation: 'Look to the mountains.' They saw a new anointing on the work there and believed that God would give them many new chapters. National FGBMFI president Jukka Koski had a vision for a hundred chapters within the succeeding five years.

It was not just northern Europe which saw this move of God. In the south of Europe, too, the Fellowship grew, perhaps a little more slowly but beginning to build up a momentum in Spain, Italy and the island of Malta. In 1992, the city of Barcelona, Spain, hosted the Olympic Games. FGBMFI gave out thousands of a special Olympic edition of *Voice* magazine during the period of the Games. These were given to spectators as well as athletes in the Olympic village. Distribution of these had begun at the US Olympic trials in New Orleans the previous June, when a thousand copies were given to American competitors. As they did later in France, the FGBMFI linked up with Lay Witnesses for Christ International and put on a banquet at a Barcelona hotel, when a number of people became Christians; the president of the Barcelona chapter, Fernando Gonzalez, was also LWCI Director for Spain. The following week they held an 'Evening with the Olympians' at the Olympic Palace of Music. Here some fifteen hundred people packed the recital hall to hear testimonies from, among others, Leroy Burrell, Mike Marsh and Carl Lewis, three-quarters of the 400-metre relay team that set a world record five days later. It is believed that some 400 million people saw parts of the event on television, and at least 200 people made commitments that night. Another very encouraging aspect of the international event was the way that so many of the different churches worked together.

John Wright took the former Abbot of Ampleforth in Yorkshire to Malta, where they received the blessing of the Archbishop and were able to set up three chapters on the island. In the late 1990s, Phil Jones and his wife Beryl, from South Wales, spent some of the winter months on the island. Phil met Joseph Aquilina, Director for Malta, and also Edward Zammitt, both of whom were anxious to encourage the new chapter on the island of Gozo. Phil agreed to travel with them to the island, but on the day they were booked to go the weather was horrendous – a terrible storm with high winds that lashed the waves on to the promenade. The hotel receptionist said they could never get to Gozo in the prevailing conditions; even if they did, there was no guarantee that they could get back. However, they set off, stopping on the way to the ferry port and asking the Lord to stop the storm so that they could get over for the luncheon meeting.

Arriving at the port they prayed again, then braved the elements to board the ferry. They sat down at a table where a young lady was already sitting, and over coffee chatted about where, and why, they were going. Suddenly something wonderful happened. The wind dropped, the rain stopped and the sea was calm to the extent that the boat did not seem to be moving at all. This young lady was most impressed – Edward had told her not to be frightened, that the Lord would give them a peaceful crossing. She went away clutching the 'A Step to Salvation' tract with her, having heard that Jesus can also calm the storms in people's lives when they make Him Lord and Saviour.

Arriving at the hotel in Mgau, Edward felt that the Lord was telling him to invite a couple, sitting in the lounge, to the luncheon. They accepted, and it turned out that they were retired Salvation Army Officers who were on the last day of their honeymoon in Gozo. They felt that the Lord had sealed their marriage with this blessing, and greatly enjoyed the time of fellowship.

When the three men returned that night to the hotel in Malta, the receptionist was amazed that they had gone to Gozo, and this amazement increased when they told her how God had answered prayer in giving them a calm crossing. As she listened, her eyes filled with tears and she asked for prayer for her sister who, with two young children, was suffering from cancer. The three men told her that they believed God would answer prayer in the name of Jesus. The other guests also enquired about the visit and were amazed at the power of prayer. This story passed from person to person, and God used it to His glory, as people came to the men with their needs and they were able to pray for them and tell them about Jesus.

In Valetta, the chapter held a fellowship meeting preceding New Year, to which Phil and Beryl were invited. They were overwhelmed by the love and devotion shown one to another. It was a family gathering as well, and they were able to pray for the children of the members of that chapter. The chapter president, a real man of God, had come to know Jesus at an FGBMFI dinner meeting as an inmate in prison. Before they returned to Wales, Beryl was able to meet the wives of the Valetta chapter, and they formed a prayer group of members' wives to meet on a regular basis.

Italy has had a number of chapters over the years, including some run by Africans and others that were international. This was due in part to the 1965 London airlift and to the work of Dr Fred Ladenius and others from Africa and the

United States. Both Demos and Richard Shakarian had been honoured by the pope for their part in helping the Catholic Charismatic Renewal. From around 1990, Luciano de Pieri, a publisher in Mantua who also led a very large charismatic group called the New Life Fellowship, was in touch with the Lugano chapter in Switzerland, but it was not until 1996 that the first Italian chapter dinner was held in Sirmione del Garda. The work was small but definitely growing, with three Italian chapters in Venice, Verona and Milan, two African chapters in Verona and Modena, and plans for two more chapters in Turin and Padua.

The first Italian national convention was held in 1998, and Apostolic Nuncio Archbishop Luigi Accogli was invited. He was not too enthusiastic, but his secretary, a sister from Ireland, encouraged him to go. At that convention, attended by Richard and Vangie Shakarian and other FGBMFI leaders from across Europe, there was an anointing of the Holy Spirit, and the Archbishop was so blessed that he stopped on his way back to Rome and telephoned the leaders at the hotel to thank the Fellowship for the privilege of attending. Since then, he has pledged himself to do all he can for the FGBMFI, and has travelled to Guatemala to speak, and to two world conventions in America.

One of the other leading men in Italy, along with Luciano, was Andrea Bovilacqua. From his early twenties, Andrea had been very successful in business. When his wife began to get involved as a catechist in the church, he joined the more social and cultural side of parish life. Both of them enjoyed their different spheres of service for ten years, until a crisis hit their family. Their youngest daughter, Francesca, was taken very ill around the time of her school-leaving exam, and was unable to graduate. For three years they tried everything that the doctors and money could provide to bring her back to health, but without success.

During this time, Andrea would sit in front of the television, trying to block the situation from his mind. One evening he watched a programme in which Indian carpets were being auctioned. He had never had any interest in these before, but found himself bidding; almost before he knew what he had done, Andrea had bought a carpet. It became like a game for him. During the bidding his heart would beat faster and he was happy when he came out the highest bidder for a prestigious carpet. Eventually he bought several hundred. Then, one day, the TV auctioneer asked to meet Andrea, as he was curious about this person who was buying so many expensive carpets. The wife of the auctioneer attended the New Life Fellowship in Peschiera del Garda, run by Luciano de Pieri, and when she heard about the problems they were having with Francesca's illness, she invited them to go along.

They were a little surprised when they saw the centre, as it was not a church or a parish hall, but in fact a converted cinema. Here, they witnessed for the first time the power of the Holy Spirit and saw the same kind of miracles Jesus had done two thousand years ago. Luciano began to pray over a period of time for Francesca, and eventually she was able to graduate. Both Andrea and his wife received the baptism of the Holy Spirit, and also a word of prophecy saying that their home would be open to many people who would want to come and find out what they had in their lives.

Andrea worked closely with Luciano to start up the Italian-speaking chapters in northern Italy, and found an avenue for service and testimony that would earlier have seemed impossible. He grasped the vision of bringing businessmen to the Fellowship and didn't hesitate to tell them they needed to go forward in the meetings to receive prayer and the anointing of the Holy Spirit. At the Spanish convention in Zaragoza, one of the meetings was on the theme of

'How to become fishers of men'. Unfortunately, there was no one present who could translate from Spanish into Italian, so Andrea prayed that he would be able to understand all the teaching, and in fact understood over 70 per cent of what was said. Since that occasion, he has travelled with Archbishop Accogli to Central America in order to share fellowship and testimony. A native of Venice, Andrea became president of the chapter in that beautiful city.

TEN

Breaking Down the Walls

Long before the collapse of Communism in Eastern Europe, God had inspired men of the Fellowship to take the Gospel to the countries behind what was known as the 'Iron Curtain'. Men from the United States organized airlifts, and from the United Kingdom groups went to Russia many times, taking Bibles and all manner of Christian teaching aids for adults and children, as well as medical supplies and other items.

As with many other former Communist countries, the food shortages and general economic problems meant it was not always possible to follow the normal pattern of FGBMFI meetings, but every opportunity was taken to get over the message that Jesus Christ is the answer to man's needs. In the early 1990s, a team from New England were able to travel to Moscow, where they witnessed to the Russian intelligentsia in groups ranging in size from 17 to 800, at universities, scientific and artistic organizations, medical facilities and hospitals, cultural centres and schools. They told what Jesus had done in their lives and shared the joys of a personal relationship with the risen Lord Jesus. The word of God was gratefully received; from 60 to 95 per cent of people at the various meetings stood to say the prayer to receive Jesus into their hearts as Lord and Saviour.

The group found that the Russians they met were open and eager to receive their good news. After each meeting, the crowds surged forward to receive more than 3,000 New Testaments in Russian that the team passed out. On many occasions, the airlift members preached Christ and prayed for salvation and healings at school and universities – something not allowed in America. Doctors, medical staff, patients, professors and highly educated professionals of all kinds asked for prayers for healings. On several occasions team members felt surges of power passing through their hands. After one meeting, a Russian professor said she felt supernatural power coming from the team as they spoke, and asked how she could come to believe in Jesus. An internationally renowned concert pianist with the Moscow Philharmonic felt the same power as the team sang praises.

There were problems! A thief broke in one night, stealing $900 in the presence of sleeping team members. Air tickets and belongings were lost or stolen, and the regular accosting in the streets by mobs of street gypsies and pickpockets were all things 'sent to try them!' However, FGBMFI men are not easily deterred, and the following year a team from northern California, led by Dario Rabak, went again to continue the work. They were thrilled at what God was doing but also sad at the sight of so much need.

We came to this children's hospital. The hospital was about 20 or 30 years old and yet there was still rubble all over the place from when they had built it. Nobody had bothered to clean it up or to landscape there. It was in a state of disrepair. None of the clocks worked. Windows were broken. Tiles were falling off the walls onto the floors and left there.

Most of the elevators didn't work. Nobody was cleaning the place properly. They didn't have anything. They didn't have light bulbs, they didn't have syringes to give injections with. They didn't have medical supplies of any kind. They didn't have diapers for the infants. They were barely able to get enough powdered milk for the infants that were born there. They are in a desperate situation.

I left my heart in that hospital.[1]

Dario appealed for whatever practical help people could give and for prayer for these children and staff. The following year he went back to Russia again, and also to the Ukraine, where the economic conditions were severe, with inflation and product shortages increasing daily, as in Russia. They found the people of the Ukraine equally open to the Christian message, seventy years of atheism having left the 300 million people of the former USSR in a moral and spiritual vacuum.

Despite the shortages, the group were involved with four dinner meetings as well as meetings on the streets, in hospitals, churches, schools, colleges and even on two television stations. They found the schools, in particular, anxious for them to go and speak to the students, who hung on to their every word. As a direct result of their efforts, three schools were open to a Bible-based curriculum. They now have Christian teachers going in on a daily basis to teach the Bible.

The first ever airlift into eastern Europe came some twelve years earlier than this, when Demos and Rose Shakarian led a team to Budapest. They had stopped over in Zurich to meet fifty plus FGBMFI men who were to be part of the airlift. Calls started coming into their hotel asking how people could come and meet them in Budapest and whether they could take the Gospel to their outlying areas of eastern Europe. The phone calls became so constant that Hungarian officials were concerned. They were worried that the men might be outside agitators stirring up their people. Because of this, the team were only allowed to visit churches, but the advantage was that instead of holding meetings in one hall in Budapest, they were allowed to travel all over the country. The government officials thought they were stopping the Americans doing what they wanted, but in fact it turned out to be a great blessing.

When they arrived at their hotel in Budapest, Demos and his team were joined by about sixty local officials. As they began eating, someone came to their table to say that a large crowed was gathering outside the hotel and they were 'waiting for Demos'. Before finishing dinner, Demos realized that God wanted them to meet the people right where they were, and so they held their first 'street meeting' in the history of the Fellowship. People were born again, healed and baptized in the Spirit, and word of this quickly spread. Wherever they went, hundreds of people came to hear the testimonies of men and women. At one meeting, over 300 stood to signify they wanted to become born again. In another meeting, a little boy who was almost completely deaf was prayed for. Demos, having been healed of deafness himself, was thrilled as the little boy was healed and ran to tell his parents. The next morning the boy's father came to the hotel while Demos was having breakfast. He was so touched by his son's healing that he wanted to give his life to Jesus.

The openness of the people of Hungary was amazing, and enabled the Spirit of God to move in power. They were told that as long as they did not speak against socialism – and they didn't – there would be no problems. One of the things they encouraged the people to do was to lift up Jesus and put the word of God into practice themselves by praying for people, for salvation and healing of the body. When Demos got back to the United States, he issued this challenge through *Voice* magazine:

Don't get complacent. This Fellowship is bigger than your individual chapter, or your regional conventions. It's a worldwide outreach. We need more of these airlifts to lands where the Full Gospel is not being preached ... it's time for the Full Gospel ministry to join hands with other Christian outreaches to harvest the millions of people waiting for the full power of God to fall on their country.

We're reaching a point in history when God will change the course of nations and the faces of continents. God showed me how He would change the faces of every continent on earth from a look of death and discouragement to a look of praise and brotherhood. Now is the time it will happen.[2]

The call for the sleeping giant of laymen to awaken was being heeded. As Demos went on to say, 'It takes thousands, tens of thousands. One man won't evangelize the world. Ten men won't do it. It takes an army.'

The Shakarian family originally came from Armenia,[3] and in the late 1980s government officials from that country started making contact with Demos, wanting him to go over. Because of the stroke he had suffered, Demos did not feel able to do this, but in 1990 Richard, with his wife Vangie, went along in place of Demos, taking with them a small group of business men.

The invitation was an official one from the government, and that opened all the doors for them to access the television, stadiums, printing and so on. The invitation had come because it was a Fellowship of business men. At that time, the country was still under the full domination of the Soviet Union and the Communist regime.

While preparing for the trip, Richard came across the prophecies given by St Gregory to the first Armenian king to accept the Lord and turn the entire nation over to

Christianity. That had been sixteen hundred years ago. Richard believed God was saying to him that if he would give the prophetic word to the men of Armenia, they would rise to the call of our Lord, just as they had done all those years earlier.

When the group arrived in Armenia, they were given royal treatment. The Christians had set up meetings, and the government, despite the fact they were Communists, gave stadiums, halls and arenas, all free of charge. Not only did the government sponsor the meetings by providing all the facilities, they paid for all the travel and accommodation while the team were in the country.

When Richard asked for the largest sports arena in the land for the final service in the capital, their reply was, 'Are you sure? There are not enough active Christian people in the whole land to fill that.' Richard insisted, and they gave it to him. From the very beginning, the power of the Lord was mighty upon the people.[4] There were 4,000 people in the first meeting. Richard spoke of the prophecy given by St Gregory in 301 AD, saying that the word of the Lord would never lose its power. He also said that, as he spoke, the Holy Spirit would speak to their spirits on the inside. Then he gave the invitation for men to respond. Tears filled their eyes as 800 men gave their lives to Jesus Christ. Young Armenian men, with men from other republics, stood there shoulder to shoulder, with their hands raised and tears pouring down their faces as they cried out to God. As Richard turned to his right, there were young Russian soldiers in full uniform, standing, weeping and beseeching God. Through the week, 10,000 men answered the call to give their lives to Jesus Christ and to evangelize the Soviet Union, as laymen to reach out for Jesus Christ.

Copies of the Gospel of John, printed by the Central Committee Communist Press and paid for by the Fellowship, were distributed – 20,000 in all, but still the people begged for more of them. Then the government officials asked what else they could do for the team, and the answer was, 'Put us on television.' The following night the group were able to share on live television how Jesus had changed their lives. On the final night, 15,000 came to the meeting, with over 4,000 more outside, banging on the doors to get in. They did not believe the stadium could be full. However, the team were able to fix up loudspeakers so that everyone outside could hear what was being said inside the stadium. That night, 6,000 people indicated that they wanted to become Christians.

When Richard and Paul Toberty, another of the business men in the group, got back to the home of one of the top officials where they were staying, the man began asking some questions. Looking them straight in the eye, he asked, 'How did you do this?' They told him they didn't understand what he meant. 'How is it that when you came to the city one week ago, you had nothing – no organization – and in one week you filled the biggest stadium we have with thousands of people? How did you do it?'

'It's very simple,' they told him. 'We didn't do it. God did! If the people are hungry for their spirits to be fed and someone says, "High on the hill overlooking the city in the stadium you will be fed and your spirit will be nourished," they will come.' The official hung his head. They were able to share what Jesus meant in their lives and asked him if he would like to receive Jesus. He said he would, and Richard and Paul were able to pray with him.

In another stadium earlier that week, filled with curious people – flags flying, Mount Ararat in the background – a great disturbance broke out. A man mute for 30 years was suddenly healed. A lady who'd been lame for 40 years was healed. For an hour and a half, it seemed as if the team were bystanders, watching God at work, as miracles abounded in that stadium. Afterwards, a well-dressed lady who was a leader in the Communist Party came up to Richard and said, 'Mr Shakarian, I'm an atheist.' Thinking she would not have stopped him just to say that, he responded, 'And?'

'I have arthritis, and haven't been able to lift up my hands or arms for many years without excruciating pain. While you were speaking I was cured.' At that point she raised her arms and Richard said, 'Now will you accept that there is a God?' She looked up at her hands in the air and said, 'Yes.' It was just like when Jesus healed the unbelieving. First came the demonstration of His power, and then the acceptance of Him.

Slowly, perhaps, at first, but surely, in the countries of eastern Europe the army of men was beginning to emerge. For many years, Jim Winter and Drew Greenwood from Scotland, at that time Directors of the Fellowship, travelled to Hungary, giving themselves tirelessly to help ground the work. Poland was establishing chapters and Dennis Spenst and his Polish-born wife Eva, from Canada, travelled there on a regular basis, helping with the translation of materials and the work in general. Romania had twelve chapters, and Daniel Nemteanu, the national president, was praying and working to see the work expanded. He too was a man who had been tremendously blessed through the Fellowship. When he became a Christian, it created a 'tremendous storm', as he puts it, in his family. His wife could not understand how he could be so full of joy and enthusiasm when life for him, and everyone else around them, was so difficult. A friend invited him to an FGBMFI prayer meeting where he not only received the baptism of the Holy Spirit but was also healed of a blood haemorrhage problem that had troubled him for many years.

When he joined the FGBMFI he was unemployed, but some months later a member from France went over and put

Daniel in touch with seven French business men. He became the manager of four French–Romanian joint ventures. He also experienced the power of healing in his family, in both his wife and daughter. Then in 1997, their son was jumping from a 10-metre high diving board; as he came off it he hit his forehead so hard with his knees that his forehead was broken. Daniel immediately took him to the hospital, but before the doctor examined the boy he prayed for healing in the name of Jesus. The doctor told them that if the bone chips had not penetrated the brain, then he would survive, but if they had, then he would be a vegetable. There was a hole in the boy's forehead and the prognosis was not good. However, within three weeks his son was totally healed, with no traces of the accident.

The work in Czechoslovakia, as it was previously known, was greatly helped for some years by the work of Malcolm Blowes and his wife from the UK. In the early 1990s an airlift was organized to encourage the men of Czechoslovakia. One of the main aims of the team was to speak in schools and churches as well as to counter the New Age teaching that was spreading so rapidly. New chapters were set up and older ones visited. Many people were brought to an experience of salvation.

Back to Hungary and the city of Budapest, where Miklos Molnar, who came from a very poor family, said he could never have imagined himself becoming a business man. In fact, at the age of 17 he became involved with the local Mafia. Starting in the hotel 'branch', within a short time he was involved in prostitution and all kinds of 'dark things'. He also began to drink heavily. For about ten years he continued this life, and then met the lady who was to become his wife, Anna. He thought that everything would change when he had someone who loved him for himself. It was only three months before he was back into his old ways.

Some five years later, Miklos met an old woman who talked to him about Jesus and how He could change people's lives. Jesus loved him, she said. This lady spoke about Jesus as if she really knew Him, which of course she did, and this impressed Miklos. One night he decided that he was so fed up with his way of life that he would give Jesus a try, so he asked Him into his life. The change was immediate. He felt like a new man and the first thing he did was to ask Anna for forgiveness. God helped him to get a good job in Austria, which gave him the opportunity not only to make a lot of money but also to get away from his old life completely.

When they returned to Budapest, Miklos asked God to help in starting up some kind of business and to show him what to do. As he prayed, God showed Miklos a picture of a one-storey building containing a number of shops. The following day he phoned a friend, and within a week plans had been drawn up and the necessary licences given. In that building he runs his own coffee and ice-cream shop.

One day someone invited Miklos to the Full Gospel Business Men's Fellowship. At first he thought these men were crazy, speaking in strange languages, but they were so clearly full of power that he allowed them to pray with him and that had a tremendous impact on him. It enabled Miklos to have a new dimension in his spiritual life that helped him to cope, even when big problems came along.

The Mafia were not happy that he had defected, and started to attack his business. They wanted a lot of money and could not understand why he refused to pay, knowing what the consequences would be – the lives of his wife and children were threatened for a period of five months – but Miklos refused to be intimidated. Finally, they came into his coffee shop one morning and sat down. They were smoking; he told them that it was not allowed in his shop and would they please put out their cigarettes. Their response was far from polite and they refused to move. Miklos realized the only thing he could do was to pray. 'In the name of Jesus, put out those cigarettes,' he said. Amazed, the men stood up, went outside and stubbed out their cigarettes, and then came back inside. Asking them to sit down again, Miklos offered them coffee and cakes and gave them his testimony. Within half an hour they were crying as the love Miklos genuinely felt for them, because of Jesus, came through his words. Now the Mafiosi come only to drink coffee and eat cakes. No one threatens his business, because they know the Mafia would not allow it!

In 1998, Miklos went over to Dallas for the world convention. He was experiencing serious financial problems and a man came over at one of the meetings and prayed with him, very simply, that Jesus would meet his needs. When he arrived back home, his wife was there to meet him, her face beaming. The day after that prayer, money owed to them but long overdue had come into the business and their financial problems were solved. Miklos said that his experiences had shown him that his place of service was in the Fellowship, and, in his words, he enjoyed the 'internationalness' of the FGBMFI. He became the national president for Hungary.

The work in Hungary, begun by Demos, continued to be built on by men from various nations, but undoubtedly the most phenomenal outreach, in 1997, was led by the International President Richard Shakarian. It came about because in the spring of that year, at a leaders' meeting in Austria for the central European countries, a member of the Hungarian parliament showed up with a TV cameraman. She had come at the invitation of Miklos Molnar. For two years, the men of the Fellowship in Hungary had gone every Tuesday morning, from six until eight o'clock, to the citadel overlooking the Danube at the parliament building. They had prayed for love and wisdom, and particularly for the parliament. Miklos had the opportunity to speak to this lady, Magdolna Volka, who was highly regarded within the Hungarian Socialist Party.

At the end of the meeting in Austria, Richard Shakarian stood up and spoke about the Good Samaritan and how it was important for the great nations who are going down the middle of the road to get down into the ditches, pick up the fallen ones and lead them into the cities to be blessed and healed. This touched a chord in Magdolna, and after the dinner that night she accepted Jesus as her Saviour. For a long time, she and her husband had wanted to start a family but she had been unable to conceive. The men prayed for her and two weeks later she conceived.

Because this woman had been so blessed by what had happened, she said she would like to bring the FGBMFI to Hungary if the parliament would make provision for a big park to enable them to have an open-air meeting with music – a real cultural event. The government was thrilled with the idea of combining business men and culture. She told them that the business men would also bring the Holy Spirit. They answered, 'Fine, bring the Holy Spirit. It's OK.'

Having been told by God to print newspapers celebrating the turning over to Christ of Hungary one thousand years earlier and containing Bible stories in tabloid form, the men from Europe and America got together to put this into effect. A hundred thousand copies of four different newspapers were printed and distributed throughout the Budapest area prior to the outreach, and resulted in many people being healed and committing their lives to Jesus even before the event started. A woman who was a translator became a Christian because of what she saw and experienced.

One day during the outreach, some of the men were giving out the newspapers in one of the squares in Budapest and went over to speak to a young man lying on a dirty rag next to a bench. He had lain there seven years begging – homeless, dirty and smelly. Having been born with a spine that was not properly fused together, he had been disabled all his life and had never been given any opportunity to do anything. One of the men showed him the paper and spoke about the story written in it. He began to pray for the young man, when suddenly the Holy Spirit led him to the passage in Acts chapter 4, which tells of how the apostles Peter and John were going up to the Beautiful Gate of the temple. Approaching the Gate, they came across a man lying by the steps who asked them for money. They told him they had none, but in the name of Jesus to rise up and walk, which he did! The man in Budapest was likewise inspired to say, 'In Jesus' name, step out and walk.' Not only did the young man stand up and walk, he ran around the square, to the astonishment of everyone. Like the man at the Beautiful Gate, he was well known because of the many years he had spent there, begging.

This amazing miracle, only one of many, made national news throughout the country, which in turn brought greater numbers to hear and see what was happening through the Full Gospel Business Men's Fellowship International.

Richard Shakarian's wife Vangie, who, like Demos' wife Rose, regularly travelled with her husband, was walking through the park before one of the meetings. She and Richard noticed two girls, who turned out to be sisters. From the way that she walked, one girl obviously suffered from cerebral palsy, and Vangie felt a real sense of compassion for her. The young girl came along to the meeting, was prayed for in the name of Jesus and wonderfully healed so that she was walking straight. The two sisters had never before heard anything about Jesus Christ. People were amazed as this girl literally grew 5 inches as she straightened up, and her sister was so overwhelmed she could not stop crying.

Ulrich von Schnurbein, from Germany, was one of the team, and he was astounded when he saw Winfried Fuchs praying with a lady who had 2-centimetre-thick glasses and could still hardly see anything. As Winfried started to pray for her, Ulrich asked the Lord to help him find a word that would build up Winfried's faith. He opened his Bible and all of a sudden saw a headline that said, 'The blind men will be healed', the story of the blind man at the Pool of Bethesda in Mark chapter 8. He showed the verse to Winfried and told him to be encouraged: the blind would be healed at that moment. The lady had come with her nephew, and as they took off her glasses, she screamed out to him, 'I can see you, I can see you!'

Some eight years earlier, God had told Richard Shakarian that He would be pouring out His Spirit in the fields. When Magdolna invited them, he felt it right to ask for a park – a field – for the last night because God had shown him that it was going to be just like it was in the time of Jesus. Richard knew that night he had to put the word of God into people. It would have to be short, with the content of a sermon and a message of testimony. The other important thing God showed him was to focus on the power of God for specific healings, and that's what happened. All of a sudden, he felt a pain in his eyes and so he called out, 'If there is anything wrong with your eyes and you are blind or can hardly see, right now God is going to heal your eyes.' Next, he felt pain in his ears, so they prayed for people who were deaf, then for blood pressure and so on. The glory of God fell on that park – it was like a rain of healing. As Richard said, when it rains, it rains on the whole field, not just parts of it, and that was what happened. It was like the book of the Acts of the Apostles, all over again.

A woman with two little children was healed of blindness, and one of her children healed from a serious breathing problem. Another lady was holding her hearing aids in her hands, able to hear normally. Others were healed of eyesight problems, crippled legs, deafness. A woman whose shoulder had been seriously damaged was completely healed, and also a young man with back problems who could not stand properly. Blair Scott reports how one older woman came up to the podium saying, 'I need help! I need help! You made a call for people who needed healing in their hearing, but I was deaf and I couldn't hear you.' They prayed for her and she was totally healed. Not satisfied with that, she said, 'I won't leave here until God heals my eyes too.' She was about 75 years old and had glasses on, quite natural for a lady of that age, but she wanted to be totally healed. She kept them there until ten o'clock in the evening, praying for her, until she said, 'God has healed me.' Rather like the story of the persistent man in the Gospels, she was determined to keep on asking until she received.

Through Miklos Molnar taking Richard for a coffee at his shop on the way from the airport, Richard was able to meet with some of the Mafia men who came there. Richard spoke to one of the men, who had a big cut on his leg and was in some pain. Suddenly he started to cry and said his leg was getting hot. The Holy Spirit touched him and the leg was healed. Later in the week, the big Mafia boss, who had heard about the healing, asked for Richard and Vangie to go and see him. Along with Miklos, Blair Scott and another member, they were able to go and witness to him and his friends about the Lord Jesus Christ. Richard felt he should tell him the story about when he had been in Armenia, and by the time he had finished, this man, who controls half of the Mafia and crime in the city, allowed them to pray for him. Richard and others were also able to meet powerful business men and leaders, meetings that they believe will bear fruit in future years.

One of the good things that came out of this outreach was the way in which so many laymen were able to come together from many different countries and work together as a team. There were no top-line evangelists or preachers, just ordinary men and women who had made themselves available for God to use. Although Richard is the International President of the Fellowship and has a tremendous gift of being able to speak to people, be they leaders of nations or beggars on the street, he too would agree that he is an ordinary man. What makes the difference for him and all the other men and women involved is that they have the anointing of God and they are willing to serve. Vangie Shakarian summed it up when she said it was about simple faith. 'A little child will step out and do things when he may not know all that's going on, but he will step out and do it because he's not afraid. That is the simplicity. When God tells us to do something, we may not know how it will all turn out, but step by step, we walk it out and God opens the door and does tremendous things.'

ELEVEN

The Far Corners of the Earth

'God needs your availability,' said Don Ostrom, president of the Seattle chapter, as he challenged the men to offer themselves to travel on airlifts for the Fellowship. This was in the mid 1970s and Bob Bignold had become the vice president of the chapter. His business was doing well and he had the money to go. For others among the men who were offering themselves, Bob knew it was a tremendous financial sacrifice. He said to his wife Barbara that he felt 'sort of cheated' because there was no problem for him. At this stage, he was still a very new Christian and had not experienced the attacks that the Devil launches when people make themselves available to spread the Gospel. By the time he left for that trip, he had been losing money for three to four months and had enough work for only half the people in the office. Bob told his wife he was going anyway, but he was going to have to trust God after all.

It might sound glamorous to be going abroad with a group of men, and sometimes women, having the opportunity of speaking to new people. But it didn't always work out that way, as Bob found. On this particular trip to Europe, he gave only a five-minute testimony in France. All that time and expense for just five minutes of speaking? However, it is what is learned on such a trip that is so important and is often preparation for what is to come in the future. This was certainly so with Bob. When he got home, Barbara said that the men in the office had called to say that while he was away, five large jobs had come in. It was as if God was showing Bob that He was the salesman, and in charge. Later he saw the significance of the trip. Bob had not thought he had done an important thing, but he had got the principle right by saying he was prepared to go even when things looked so bad in the office.

Most men of the Fellowship found that once they had been abroad, be it with a large or small group, it brought a sense of belonging to, and being a part of, this great international movement. Bob went to Honduras and started a chapter there, and then sat back for a year or two until he was invited to go on an airlift to Ireland. About two weeks before he left, there was a feeling in his spirit about Japan, and Bob wondered if he had missed it by going to Ireland. However, when he got on the plane one of the men turned to him and said, 'We have to go to Japan next year.' He knew that was the confirmation he needed. As soon as he got back to Seattle from Ireland, he told Phil Israelson that they had to go to the Orient, and announced that there would be an airlift at their convention. A lady who was in that meeting rang up and told Bob that she had names of people in Japan who were Christians and who would be able to assist the men. That was the beginning of regular visits over more than ten years, up to the present, of going to Japan every year, not just once but often two or three times.

Japan was a very different story from other nations to which Bob had arranged airlifts. It was hard going and required a tremendous commitment. One of the first things they had to learn about was Japanese courtesy. They would find Christians and talk to them about being leaders, and the people would say, 'Yes, yes,' but they didn't mean 'yes'. It was just their way, and Bob began to feel frustrated because they seemed to be making so little headway. Eventually they met a New Zealander who said he would set up meetings and invite all the Christian leaders to come, and Bob would be able to share his testimony. It's wonderful the way God solves not just one problem, but often two or more, in a situation. Bob didn't know, but this New Zealander had become very disillusioned about healing, even though he had been raised in a church which believed and taught it. After Bob finished his testimony, he asked anyone with pain or sickness in their body to come up to the front, because God would heal them. At first he could not get anyone to come up, because the Japanese were afraid of losing face, but eventually a man came who had pains in his stomach; after prayer, they disappeared. A lady who had pain came forward and was healed. Then Bob felt the faith drain out of him as he saw an old lady come up, dragging her leg, in which the muscles had atrophied over the previous five or six years. Knowing he had no choice, he just closed his eyes and prayed. God instantly restored the muscles and she jumped up and down. Of course, everyone wanted prayer after seeing such a miracle! The man who was so disillusioned about healing was now faced with the truth. God can and does heal.

It took about two years before the Seattle men managed to get a Japanese to become a chapter president, but from this slow beginning God built up the work, and the men from Seattle, and other places, kept on going. Bob was made to realize that there is often a price to pay. The year after his first trip to Japan, he lost 45 per cent of his wealth. The following year, for a quarter of the time, it was difficult to make the payroll each month. Eventually, he began to realize that the business problems were connected with his travelling to Japan. One night, when he thought he was broke, he went up into the loft of the house and said to God, 'I don't know what or how I am going to do it, but I want You to know that I am going to keep on doing Your work and going to Japan.' God honoured that and turned his business around in a supernatural way.

For six months there was no change in the business. One day, Bob was at breaking point – his bookkeeper told him on the Monday that they would not have enough money for the payroll. In faith, he spoke out and said to her, 'You are about to see a miracle of God.' No sooner were the words out of his mouth than he heard the Devil say, 'And what are you going to tell her next week when you cannot make the payroll?' That week was one of the worst of his life. He got home on the Friday evening and said to Barbara that there was an FGBMFI meeting at the airport hotel and he needed to go to get some encouragement. When he arrived, they sat him down at the head table; none of the people had any idea of what he was going through. When the speaker that night had finished his testimony, he said, 'I command the Spirit of doubt and unbelief to go. God is big enough to bring in your payroll next week, and the week after that, and the week after that.'

Bob was beginning to understand the importance of actively speaking out faith in the word of God, in the promises of God, and proclaiming what God was going to do, even when the natural situation seems to be everything to the contrary. His business held steady; one month later, when he called into the office, they had just been awarded the largest design job from the navy. They sold six times more work in that year than in any other. Someone once gave Bob a definition of faith: 'Faith is information we get from God to act on. Faith is a noun and belief is a verb.' It is saying, as Bob did, 'God, even though I am going broke, nothing will make any difference to our relationship.'

Kenchi Tsukamoto was now the International Director for FGBMFI in Japan, as well as being the president for that country. He acknowledged how the Fellowship had changed his life because of the anointing of the Holy Spirit. Since he had become a member, he had been able to lead many people to Jesus and into the baptism of the Holy Spirit. After Ken became a Christian, he did not like people who had a 'Pentecostal' or 'Charismatic' experience, until one day a pastor from Korea came to a church near where he lived. It was like a spiritual culture shock. This pastor looked so happy that his face was shining with joy. He told the people that he had not always been like that, but the baptism of the Holy Spirit had made all the difference. Ken decided that he wanted to be like this pastor, and if that meant having to have the baptism of the Holy Spirit, then so be it. Although he was prayed for that night, he did not experience anything, but later in the year he had the opportunity to visit Pastor Yongi Cho's church in Korea, and it was there that he had a tremendous experience of receiving the power of the Holy Spirit, giving him the ability and desire to share his Christian faith as never before. Unfortunately, as Ken knew, there are very few opportunities in oriental countries such as Japan for laymen to be able to minister. Pastors and full-time ministers think it is their job, and laymen are not supposed to get too involved. They told Ken if he wanted to minister he would have to attend a Bible School, but as he was already a school teacher he decided to continue with that work. Little by little, the fire and enthusiasm inside him died.

In the mid 1980s, a group of business men from Seattle visited his church. This was, of course, the FGBMFI, led by Bob Bignold. After Ken heard Bob share testimony, he got another culture shock. He wondered what kind of people they were that a layman could speak in such a powerful way and pray for the sick. His prayer was, 'Lord, I want to be like them. I want to be like brother Bob.'

Whenever the men from Seattle came to his home town of Kobe, Ken would attend the meetings, continuing to be amazed that laymen were praying for salvation, healing and deliverance, in fact whatever the people needed. Soon he became a member and started a chapter in Kobe, so happy to have at last found a place to work for the Lord. At first, he saw his role as running the chapter and organizing meetings for the men coming from abroad, but eventually he too, step by step, started to give his testimony and pray for people. At first he was very nervous and felt perhaps he shouldn't be doing it, but the Lord trained and anointed him. Eventually he was able to speak at chapters, conventions and churches, and to see people saved and healed and delivered from evil spirits. He received a prophecy that told him that he would minister in many countries and pray for leaders in the world. In Ken's mind there was no way this could happen, but in 1997 he met President Ramos of the Philippines and, along with Richard Shakarian, found himself praying for him.

Each year an annual convention was held in Japan that attracted pastors and people from all over the country and from abroad. In 1997, six men and women from Zaire made the trip. That year, a highlight of the convention was a narration by the well-known Japanese artist, Toyotake Hanabusadayu, entitled, 'Behold the Man', in the ancient Japanese *Gidayu Bunraku* artform. This traditional Japanese art requires the artist to study under a master for twenty years before he is considered a professional. The play, which was specially written by Hanabusadayu, depicted the life and crucifixion of Jesus and, for the first time in the 250-year history of *Bunraku*, the narration was spoken in English. Toyotake was a member of the Osaka chapter.

It may have been difficult, it may have cost men a great deal in many ways, but God was honouring His call upon the lives of individuals to establish this part of His work in what was considered to be the most difficult country to evangelize.

Back in the 1960s, Enoch Christoffersen, mayor of Turlock, California, and an International Director of the FGBMFI, organized conventions in Japan. He also personally financed the publication of *Voice* in Japanese. Many times in the history of the Fellowship, it would seem that countries were opened up only to close again, but the foundation is there, and in God's time, as with Japan, other men are able to come along and build on what has been done in the past.

Through the FGBMFI men, many other countries of the Far East were also touched by God. Two men from Washington State, Julius Templeton and Don Snow, visited Mongolia. For four months the previous year, Don had travelled across the country showing the film *Jesus*. Before he left, he had been able to make contacts in the military that enabled them, on the following visit, to meet the Minister of Defence, through whom they were hoping to receive permission to teach military officers ethics based on the Bible. Just before the two men left America, a friend of Julius' rang to tell him not to 'water down' their purpose for being in Mongolia.

When they arrived in Ulan Bator, a diplomat who was to be their interpreter met them at the airport. They believe that this man was only the fifth person in Mongolia to become a Christian. He too advised them to be up front about the biblical basis of the seminar, which, of course, confirmed the word Julius had been given. They spoke to the Minister of Defence, along with two hard-line Communist generals, and miraculously received permission to hold a three-day seminar for up to a hundred military officers. Time was available to visit some of the people in their homes, houses made of felt with no bathrooms or running water.

Julius was to return again in 1999, when he would be stopping off in China, and he along with others of the Fellowship prayed that more doors would be opened in these countries.

Over a number of years, John Carrette from Guatemala, the Executive Vice President of the Fellowship, visited China. Around 1993, some Chinese men came to the headquarters in California and told Richard Shakarian that they were there because of a prophecy they had heard in China over the previous four years. It was the same prophecy that was being heard throughout the churches in China, that it was time for China to evangelize the nations. Not being able to leave their country, they were able to speak to a group from Taiwan who knew about the FGBMFI. At that time, China was beginning to open up, and they thought that maybe, rather than going out as missionaries, they would go out as business men. This was why these men from Taiwan had come to California.

Richard asked John Carrette to go with these men, and since 1995 he has been able to develop a relationship with them as he has gone two or three times a year, travelling to all parts of China. Obviously it was thought that chapters would be set up, but as so many of the churches were not able to be out in the open, John began to ask questions. 'What was the thing that the Chinese Church was afraid of?' The answer was perhaps a surprising one. They were afraid of freedom.

John realized that they did not need another layer on the Church at this time. FGBMFI was primarily needed to be a service to the Church, to encourage and support it in what it was already doing and, when the time comes, to be able to help the Chinese fulfil their call to evangelize the nations. They pay a high price for being Christians, none more so, in the way in which they are ostracized and even imprisoned.

One day, John's wife Charlotte asked him what it was like going to China. His response was: 'It is like going home. The Lord has put these people on my heart.'

'Fires have been lit in India which we pray will spread throughout the nation.' These words are from a report by Dr Graham Tipple, regarding his visit to Delhi with Eric Bardell and two other men, originally from Brazil. Graham had to visit New Delhi in connection with his work at Newcastle University, where he lectured, and hearing that Eric was hoping to make an outreach visit, they were able to combine their efforts. It was a difficult time for Christians in northern India, where being baptized in the name of Jesus led to terrible persecution. Despite this, God wonderfully showed His power.

When they arrived in March 1999, they met their two contacts now living there, and an outreach meeting was held, when 128 of what were described as 'the cream of Delhi business men believers' came in response to telephone calls from Josh, one of the men based in that city. The buffet dinner was paid for by FGBMFI in the UK. Those who attended ranged from one of the top Air India people at Indira Gandhi International Airport, who often flew with, and had the ear of, the Indian prime minister, to senior civil servants, a High Court advocate, teachers and business men across a range of industries. Only 15 of them were ministers. Fifty churches and one seminary were represented. Very unusually for India, the people arrived early!

Eric chaired the meeting and, helped by a first-class worship team and interpreter, for over two hours, with intervals for worship, they presented the FGBMFI. They explained about the Fellowship, its origins and vision, its structure, how it works and so on. Emphasis was laid on its importance as a great lay organization, releasing men into ministry, and how God has used it to impact nations. Graham was able to speak about the effect of FGBMFI in the countries he had visited, Lauro spoke about it in his home country of Brazil, and Eric about the Argentine and the Philippines. 'The anointing,' said Graham, 'was tangible.' The buzz and excitement as they sat down to the meal was electric. The men were excited and wanted to start chapters.

Thirty business men came to a meeting three days later. For this, Eric had prepared a very detailed set of guidelines on starting a new chapter. They were so 'spot on' that Graham thought they had come from headquarters, but Eric assured him that he had written them only that day! 'God can use lawyers, too!' said Graham. *The Happiest People on Earth* and *Voice* magazines were given out, and one of the men offered his house for a meeting in order to set up a chapter and organize an outreach dinner, to be held in December of 1999.

One of the Indian business men shared with them how he believed India needed FGBMFI. He said there were missions in India to the poor, the villages, the lepers and to other needy groups of people, but he had been asking and praying for years about how to reach the upper and middle classes, and the business community. God had answered and brought the FGBMFI!

Because the Indian Church was experiencing such severe persecution, Lauro told them how the FGBMFI had helped transform the Church in Brazil from a poor downtrodden Church to a rich Church, a sending Church, one with national influence that people thought twice about interfering with, because now there were many Christian MPs.

There were nearly one billion people in India, the second largest population of any country in the world. It was only just opening up its trade links with the rest of the world; the former anti-Christian government had fallen, and the country needed prayer. 'I can remember no India-shaped hole mentioned in Demos' vision of men praising God,' said Graham. 'There is no reason to assume India should miss out on the blessing, so let's go for it and get involved.' For Eric Bardell the trip was an answer to prayer. He had been travelling, building up relationships and ministering in India since

1994. Despite his strong desire to set up chapters, the openings had not previously been there, but God's timing is always right. There were now five flourishing chapters in Assam.

Jerome Wagenius, from Seattle, also travelled to India on a regular basis, to the city of Hyderabad. The name means 'bad water', and he could testify that it certainly was! He talked about the problems of poverty and the bondage of the Indian people to their many religions. Along with Dr Ernest Komanapalli, Jerome spent fourteen days speaking and ministering in hospitals, orphanages and one leper colony. As in Hungary and other places, dramatic healings drew the crowds. One night a man with three large growths on his stomach was completely healed, and such was the pressure of people wanting prayer that Jerome needed two full circles of men with arms joined around him to hold back the needy crowd and prevent him being crushed. They were looking to begin a number of chapters in that part of India and would be travelling again in the near future.

Until recently, the last FGBMFI airlift to Vietnam was to American soldiers during the Vietnam War. On that occasion they were met by Merlin Carothers, now the well-known author of *Prison to Praise* and other titles, at that time an army chaplain. Thirty years later, a number of FGBMFI men tried to establish Christian contacts and set up meetings, but without success. Just three and a half weeks before leaving, they met a Vietnamese pastor from their city and he was able to set up contacts for them. They had heard that it would be unwise to take in Bibles other than their personal copies, and because this was to be the first of many trips, they felt it important to keep a low profile and attempt to do everything they could to comply with the current laws.

As they travelled to different meetings, one day with dust masks and caps to cover their identity while travelling on the back of motorcycles, they were able to share the vision of why they were in Vietnam. In turn, the Vietnamese told them some dramatic stories, including one of a young evangelist who ran out of fuel while in the highlands. He poured water into his fuel tank and prayed, asking Jesus to turn the water into petrol, and He did! From that first visit, a chapter was set up which grew to 25 members. The work there was continuing.

God was also blessing the work of the Fellowship in Indonesia, where there were by now many chapters and hundreds of members. It was exciting that the members there were initiating airlifts to cities in remote parts of their country. Thailand was seeing a great revival, and in the Philippines, too, the number of chapters was growing. President Humberto Lotilla believed that the fresh anointing that came on the Fellowship in these years was having its impact in their corner of the world. During the period Ramos was the president of the Philippines, Richard Shakarian and well-known speaker and writer Mel Tari travelled there to spread the Gospel and encourage the work of the Fellowship. The president appreciated the work of the FGBMFI and wanted it to be even more involved in that nation. Richard and Mel Tari travelled to Java, Malaysia and Singapore before going on to the Philippines. At a great banquet held in Manila, those who attended were the 'Who's Who' of the country. Eight or nine generals from the forces were present, as were the president's secretary, the owner of the largest paper in Manila and other key leaders in the country, including five governors. Many people were born again that night, and others healed. One of those was Vice Governor Villegas, then the FGBMFI president in Manila. He was the man who had organized the banquet for around 400 people. A rather large man, he'd had problems with his leg, and after prayer he started jumping around to such an extent that the stage was rocking. Another man healed that night was the Mexican Consul General to the Philippines, and yet another was healed from a cataract. One governor said that since the Fellowship began, this was probably the most exciting, anointed, powerful meeting he had ever attended, and that the impact would go a long way in helping the growth of FGBMFI throughout Asia.

TWELVE

Down Under

'This thing has the greatest potential in the market-place of anything you have ever seen.'

As has been the case in many countries, *Voice* magazine was responsible for people first hearing about the Full Gospel Business Men's Fellowship International in Australia. In the early 1960s, a man from Melbourne attended a booksellers' convention in the USA and returned to Australia with a handful of these magazines, which he sent out to people in Adelaide, Brisbane, Sydney and Perth. From this a chapter was set up in Adelaide, followed by Brisbane, then Sydney, Melbourne and Perth.

Bernie Gray was a Christian business man with five companies in Brisbane. He and six or seven other men met together for three or four months to pray, and they tried to work out how you have a meeting. They read *Voice* magazines to see what others did, appointed a chairman, secretary and treasurer, and put on a meal in a swimming pool complex. Bernie says that when he went along, 'I was the most embarrassed guy in Australia.' He was in the motor industry in a big way, very well known in the city, and later had his own plane and pilot. When they arrived at the venue the treasurer was ready to take the cost of the meal – 7s 6d (old money) – but he had turned up with a 7lb syrup tin into which he dropped the coins, and they were making such a clanging noise that Bernie wanted to crawl under the table.

Worse was to come! When it came to the offering time, the treasurer tipped the money collected for the meal out on to the table, put it in his pocket, then proceeded to take up the offering in the syrup tin! Going home from the meeting, Bernie was getting all wound up inside about it and said to the Lord, 'What is this all about?' No sooner were the words out of his mouth than God said, 'Get rid of your filthy pride. This thing has the greatest potential in the market-place of anything you have ever seen.'

Bernie did get rid of his 'filthy pride' and became whole-heartedly involved in the work of the Fellowship, travelling to open new chapters and organizing conventions. In 1978 he visited the USA with a group of men and went back from the FGBMFI headquarters with several tapes of *Good News* programmes. He had been involved with this project in America, interviewing most of the Australian men with him for the programmes. He was determined that they should be aired on Australian TV; following his negotiations with American Video International and Channel 9, they were given time on the network every Sunday morning for a half-hour programme. The stations applauded the programme because it was not 'pulpit preaching' but ordinary men telling their stories.

The cost of converting the videos to the Australian system and then airing them each week was very high, but the FGBMFI was congratulated by Channel 9 as being the only Christian programme that paid its bills on time. In South Australia and Victoria, *Good News* was shown for three years in Brisbane and for four and a half years in Perth. This high profile was a great help in the rapid growth of the Fellowship in the 1980s.

When the World Expo was held in Brisbane, the Fellowship in Australia initiated the 'Pavilion of Promise' outreach, a $3.4 million project led by Bernie Gray. With this project some 1,250 churches became involved, and each of them put up a sign at the church entrance indicating their support for this outreach. Visitors were presented with the Gospel of Jesus Christ in a unique way, and it was very successful.

For many years, Bernie was the national president of the Fellowship in Australia. He has always believed that the Fellowship should become involved not only with churches but with the civic and political leaders. He encouraged the men to pursue this avenue, which resulted in a Governor's Breakfast in Perth. At first only 30 to 40 people came, but now there isn't a ballroom or hotel big enough to cater for all the people who want to come. They regularly have 650 people and have to turn between 200 and 400 away.

Another Australian innovation is to go to colleges and secondary schools, inviting the captains of the schools, through the heads and the parents, to be guests of the chapter at that particular function. At the last breakfast, there were 34 captains from various schools present. The students are expected to give a report in an open session when they go back to school and the Fellowship receives a lot of response from heads and parents.

Realizing the importance of getting Christian principles into young students, Bernie Gray and his son conducted vocational and career nights at the schools. They arranged for men to go to these evenings in different schools, where they would explain what it meant to them to be FGBMFI members and talk about Christian ethics in business. They firmly believed that the only balance in any community was the strength of the Christian community. If there was no strong Christian community, then you had a pagan community. It was therefore crucial to get Christian influence into every aspect of life, including civic and educational events, and because Full Gospel is made up of business men, this gave it credibility.

In 1992, Allan Jones, then a Director in the UK, visited Australia and Fiji, and just reading the places and dates of his visits there is exhausting.[1] Allan had visited the area on previous occasions, but this time spent about seven weeks constantly travelling, sharing testimony, preaching, praying for the sick and being a great encouragement to all the men of the Fellowship. Many hundreds of people came to know Jesus, hundreds were baptized in the Holy Spirit and many people healed physically, emotionally and in their marriages. In one meeting in Fiji, where about 80 people were present, 16 came forward for salvation and many were healed. One young man had been in an accident and was unable to use one of his legs. The Lord healed him so that he was able to run and jump. Allan was particularly blessed by a man called Seru, who was the chapter president in Suva, the capital of Fiji. The chapter met in a Chinese restaurant; other functions were being held there too, so screens were put around the 50 or so people attending the FGBMFI dinner, but, of course, everyone was able to hear what was being said. Seru led the meeting, singing with a guitar and giving a short testimony. He was the Attorney General of Fiji, and a friend with him was a member of the Senate. Two of the staff were prayed for and received healing.

The work in Fiji was an excellent example of how well-known business men and politicians could play a leading role in the Fellowship. Bernie Gray travelled there for many years, and a South Pacific convention was held there. A luncheon was put on for invited political and business leaders. Seru, who was also national president, was there, as well as a former

Attorney General. Just before the lunch, this man rang to ask if he could bring his wife along. She was a haemophiliac; she had had some teeth out three weeks before and had still not stopped bleeding. It was clear that her husband was afraid she would die. The men prayed – just a short prayer. She went out to the washroom to rinse out the towel she had over her mouth and found that the bleeding had stopped.

When the meal came around, this same lady said she hadn't eaten a proper meal for over eight months because of problems with her throat, and asked them to take her food away. She had a dress on which was buttoned right up to the neck, most unusual in that heat, and so the men asked again if she was all right. In answer, she opened the neck of her dress to reveal a large goitre. Again, prayer was made on her behalf, and immediately, in the name of Jesus, the goitre disappeared. She then asked for her meal back and ate every bit of it. Her husband could hardly believe his eyes. This man, although having held high position in the islands as a former Attorney General, was a drunkard, ashamed of himself because he would sometimes be found in the streets, having passed out with the amount of drink. When the appeal for salvation was made at the end of the lunch, he was the first man to put up his hand. He then went to Seru, the current Attorney General, and said, 'Anything you want help with to get this Fellowship going, I will do it.' Apart from one small relapse shortly after that, the man is now totally free from alcohol addiction and his wife says he is like a new man. As a barrister, he got lawyers, medical doctors and justice fraternity men together every Friday evening, and they looked at the issues facing the government in the forthcoming week. They then looked into the Bible to find the answers.

The same man told Bernie Gray that an Australian group in Fiji wanted to bring in casinos and gaming rooms. His responsibility was to bring the documents and draft them for the Attorney General. Bernie wondered what he should say and quietly asked the Lord for wisdom. Then he said, 'Sir can I ask you a question? How does the government deal with welfare in this country?' His response was that you either worked or you had to steal. Bernie then said, 'Would you like to thrust this country into a damage control situation, and make it worse for the people who are poor, because they will be targeted?' So there were no casinos, and no gaming rooms. Such openings were the reason why Bernie and other men from Australia believed it was important to get in touch with political figures.

In Papua New Guinea, he became friendly with the prime minister. When he visited the island of Tonga, Bernie would call the secretary to the king, who was able to set up itineraries for him. This meant he and other FGBMFI men got to meet with the ambassadors to the various countries, police commissioners and important business men.

Members in Australia were also concerned with the opposite end of the spectrum, the prisons. Jon Terpstra is a director of the Fellowship in New South Wales. In 1991 he was bankrupt, in his words, 'reduced from a stretch limousine to a train ticket'. Born in Holland, he married a Christian girl, Marty, and they had a baby daughter who was a great joy to them. At seven months old, she died in a cot death. They decided to migrate to Australia and make a new start.

Jon became very successful, working in the promotional design world, and had accounts running into hundreds of thousands of dollars, but things started going badly wrong when the businesses of two main clients collapsed. The domino effect came into play, and for three years Jon was fighting court cases. He finished up losing everything. 'By that time I was very angry, hated my wife, the girls and the church, but I didn't show it and, being a creative guy, devised a plan to get back at everyone.'[2]

He took on a new identity and made a new world, working as a freelance art director under a new name. Jon was playing a double game but nobody knew, not his wife, his church friends nor former business colleagues. He lied to everyone and used to sit in church and pity those around him who didn't know how clever he was. 'In 1988 I helped design some books, including the *Australian Heritage Cookbook*, which within eight months had sold over a million copies. I moved away from Marty and the family. They didn't know about my double life even then.'[3]

The company became successful world-wide, and Jon (then known as Don) was living life in the fast lane. He was a member of the rich set around Sydney and many other places in the world, often shouting free drinks at most of the clubs and hotels. Sometimes he tipped the doorman, the barman or anyone serving amounts up to $1,000. This went on until 1989. Then he was caught out by his daughter when he was in the mountains at Katoomba with other women. His response was to tell his wife that since she had found him out she could keep everything, and he walked out. Kerensa and Kirsten, his two daughters, ran after him, calling him back, and to his amazement he began to cry.

'Train up a child in the way he should go, and when he is old he will not depart from it', says Proverbs 22:6. Events began to catch up with Jon, as did God's word, planted in his heart so many years ago. Scriptures kept coming into his mind, and when he found his business partners using astrology to guide their decisions on how to handle him, he was very angry.

Gradually and hesitatingly, Jon made contact with his estranged wife Marty again. She agreed to go out. She said she and two other ladies had been praying for him constantly for seven years because 'she didn't want me to go to hell, she wanted me to go to heaven'. Jon went to a seminar that led him to deal seriously with God and His truth. He knew he had to change his life but he wasn't sure how. In 1991 he became, in his words, 'a real Christian'. He was completely honest with his wife about his past life, and although it was a very difficult time God brought them through. The following year a friend sponsored him for a Christian event called the 'Emmaus walk', where Jon experienced a close encounter with the healing love of God. At that event, he met an FGBMFI man who invited him to the Sydney Hills chapter. Immediately he became a member and soon a chapter president.

Part of his ministry in the FGBMFI was in the prisons. Having heard the testimony of a prison chaplain at their dinner, he was able to begin to get involved, and started the first chapter inside a prison in Australia. At the beginning of that ministry, Jon was introduced to Jeffry, a ring-leader in Parramatta Prison. They had a two-hour conversation sharing their life experiences, and Jon told him what the Lord had done in his life. They had both been millionaires, so they had things in common. The 4 p.m. bells were sounded, a sign for the prisoners to go into their cells to be locked up, and as Jeffry went, Jon said he and Marty would pray for him that night. Jeffry, who did not believe in God, said, 'You do what you like,' and left.

Faithful to his promise, Jon and Marty prayed for the prisoner that night, that God would not give him rest until he surrendered his life. They then went away for the weekend, but two days after their return received a fax from the prison ministry co-ordinator asking Jon to come into the prison as soon as he could: Jeffry wanted to see him urgently. As he arrived at the entrance to the meeting area, which happened to be the prison chapel, Jeffry started to yell, 'Please forgive me.' Jon wondered what was the matter, as there was nothing to forgive in his case. Jeffry's face had totally changed and he now had a happy, peaceful expression. All Jon could say was, 'What's happened to you?'

Jeffry told him how, after he went back to his cell, he kept wondering to himself why 'that idiot', whom he didn't know, would want to pray for him. Try as he might, Jeffry was unable to shake off this thought, and in the middle of the night he got down on his knees, confessed all his sins and became a child of God. He couldn't sleep then, because of the excitement he felt, and he wanted to be able to see all those whom he'd harmed in any way to ask their forgiveness – especially the clergy, to whom he'd been a real nuisance. Two years later, Jeffry became the first prison chapter president in Australia.

An airlift from the United States was responsible for starting the work in New Zealand in 1969. The first chapter was set up in Auckland with Jack Jensen as president. He was still actively involved in the Fellowship in 1999. Other chapters quickly followed in Hamilton, Hawkes Bay, Horowhenua and Nelson, until there were 50 active chapters operating right through New Zealand. These included two prison chapters. Members of the FGBMFI in New Zealand were active in sending airlifts overseas, particularly to the Pacific islands, where chapters were also established.

One of the leading ministries to come out of New Zealand was that of Bill Subritzky. His conversion to Christianity was a result of his daughter coming into contact with the Fellowship. When he met and wanted to marry his wife Pat, the vicar insisted that he took a course of instruction in the Christian faith. The six weekly sessions always ended in violent theological arguments; Bill, being a lawyer, was good at 'stating' his case. When the instruction finished and he was able to marry, Bill determined he would never again darken the door of a church – always a dangerous thing to say – but his desire to be socially mobile pushed him into accepting positions on church committees that required his attendance at the services on a reasonably regular basis.

'I was working hard for God. I wasn't sure there was a God, by the way, but if there was then I considered that he was lucky to have me on his side!'[4] This was Bill's assessment of his life. Successful in business, he was beginning to acquire the necessary trappings of wealth – Rolls-Royce, substantial land holdings, expensive home – but the more he succeeded the worse became his marriage and family relationships. About this time, a Full Gospel Business Men's Fellowship member, Enoch Christofferson, was booked to preach in Bill's local church. Bill's younger daughter Maria and wife Pat went to hear him, and were greatly impressed. Maria, wise to her father's ways, knew how to get his attention, so she told Bill casually that this man was a multi-millionaire. That made him listen, and he asked how this guy had made his money. Maria told him, 'Selling turkeys'. Not only that, she said, he also spoke in tongues. It was all too much for Bill – 'a tongue-talking turkey millionaire!' But he couldn't deny the change in his daughter, who had asked Jesus to come into her life and had been baptized in the Holy Spirit. She constantly prayed for her parents, whose marriage was almost at an end.

One night, Bill was faced with the reality of the healing power of Jesus Christ when he saw a woman he knew well healed from arthritis. Pat persuaded him that they should both go for prayer as they had problems with their knees, having done a lot of snow and water skiing. Bill insisted they waited until everyone else had gone, and he then reluctantly agreed to be prayed for. Within a month, his cartilages had been healed and that condition never returned. Miracles seemed to be happening everywhere he went. Finally, one day, after he quietly slipped up his hand in church, his daughter Maria came and whispered to him, 'Dad, come and get baptized in the Holy Spirit.' It was the last barrier and the final confirmation that God was real. As he began to speak in tongues, Bill realized he had to give his whole life over to Jesus and he did, lock, stock and barrel.

For many years following his conversion, Bill ministered powerfully in the Full Gospel Business Men's Fellowship International, giving testimony and seeing amazing miracles of healing and deliverance. He has spoken a number of times at the FGBMFI world convention as well as throughout New Zealand and other countries.

In 1979, Demos Shakarian asked Joash Waihura of Guadalcanal, Solomon Islands, part of Papua New Guinea, to set up an FGBMFI chapter there. But not until 1999 did the help he needed arrive. At the FGBMFI world convention in 1996, Bob Nations prayed about where a new chapter was needed. He saw in a vision the words 'Solomon Islands' flashing across a movie marquee. He set out from St Louis in April with his wife, Bonnie, and daughter, Holly. Stopping first in Australia, they became the first passengers ever to tell one taxi driver about Jesus. The man was saved and filled with the Holy Spirit, and began speaking in other tongues.

After they had arrived on Guadalcanal, the largest of the Solomon Islands, they were invited into the home of Sir Peter Keniloa, a former prime minister. His wife took them to the school where she taught, and they prayed for the children and for the teachers. Sir Peter attended the FGBMFI introductory meeting, at which there were ten business men who 'caught the vision of reaching their fellow business men with shared testimonies at luncheons. They saw it not as another organization or club, but truly as something that could change their Islands.'

The report of this event from the Seattle chapter's *Airlift Herald* told how Bob and his family learned that Joash Waihura, then over 60 years old, was travelling about, evangelizing his people without owning a car, a boat or even a phone. Perplexed as how they could find him, Bob asked the assistant of a small shop if she knew this man. Out of the 150,000 people they could have asked, she just 'happened' to live next door to Joash. They visited his home and were greeted with flower leis and a song of welcome that melted their hearts. Two hundred people came together and there were healings and deliverances taking place, one after the other. It was all God – He had all of their answers. Just before they left the islands, Bob and his family had the opportunity to lead another taxi driver, as well as several people at their hotel, to the Lord and to receive the baptism of the Holy Spirit.

In the world convention in Anaheim, July 1999, Tim Storey was preaching one evening. At the end of his message he began to call people out for words of prophecy or healing, and the first three people he asked to come forward were a man sitting on the platform, a lady on the right side of the room and a young lady on the left of the room. He then gave each of them a word of prophecy. Tim Storey had no idea that these three people were Bob Nations, his wife, Bonnie, and his daughter, Holly.

In the mid 1990s, two young men from the Solomon Islands came over to study at the college in Grimsby, UK. A friend took them along to the church attended by Dorothy and Bill Proudfoot, members of the local FGBMFI chapter, whose daughter and son-in-law were working in the Solomon Islands. One of the young men, Ken, was already a Christian. He had lost his wife shortly before coming over to the UK, and had left his daughter living with his mother-in-law. As he talked to the Proudfoots, they discovered that the person she worked for, as housekeeper, was Dorothy and Bill's daughter. Ken and his friend were invited to the FGBMFI Grimsby dinner the following Monday, when Ken was baptized in the Holy Spirit and the other young man, Edward, was born again. Shortly after this, both these young men returned to the islands.

At an Australian national convention, when Richard Shakarian was one of the speakers, he was overwhelmed with the love and fellowship he experienced and by the vision of the men to reach Australia and the South Pacific. Not long after he returned home, one of the Australian men came to see Richard in the international headquarters in California. He arrived late in the afternoon and brought his taxi driver up to the office with him. He told Richard, 'This taxi driver loves God, but he needs the baptism of the Holy Spirit.' He also told Richard about the latest outreach to Papua New Guinea, when the Holy Spirit came upon people in one meeting and they could literally see tongues of fire, just as the book of Acts describes. Following the outreach, church attendance is reported to have doubled for the whole island.

Tony Urich was a member of the Frankston chapter in Victoria. One day when driving through Brisbane, he felt an intense pain in one of his eyes. At the next suburb he stopped at a shop, and the people inside asked him what was wrong with his eye, as it was very red. Looking in a mirror, he realized it was a recurrence of a long-standing problem. On reaching a friend's house at Logan he was advised to get prompt medical attention. The doctor said that this problem would dissipate after about a week, but that he had a cataract on his eye. This was confirmed after a second examination.

Returning to Melbourne, Tony went to an FGBMFI meeting and mentioned that he was to see a specialist the next day for treatment to the cataract. There and then, members prayed for healing. Next day the specialist said, 'Who told you you have a cataract? Your eyes are perfect.' Prior to this, Tony had also had a problem of split vision and felt grit in his eyes all the time. Since the prayer by members of the chapter, his eyes are now perfect. 'The Lord in His goodness and mercy healed everything, not just the cataract.'[5]

Australian FGBMFI had its eye on the Olympics of 2000. They started an athletics club in preparation to enable them to go inside the Olympic village and be able to witness to the athletes from all nations.

These testimonies are further examples of how the vision of the Fellowship is working throughout the world. The 'awakening giant' of laymen was made up of ordinary people, beginning to realize their potential in God. Often it was only a small thing, but it could have far-reaching consequences. The man who invited Jon Terpstra to a dinner would have no idea of how God was going to use Jon in the Fellowship. Bernie Gray had to accept 7lb syrup tins and forget his pride, with all that this has meant for the work of FGBMFI in Australia and the islands.

THIRTEEN

'Oh Africa – You're in My Heart'

As a young boy, he lay on his bed and stared into the dark night. Phantom faces leered at him as he clutched the covers tightly around his neck to protect himself, but it seemed as if his breath was being cut off. Struggling, he eventually fought free, fled the room and then ran out of the house into the dark street. From the age of 10 until he was 16, these encounters with evil forces plagued Kwabeno Darko. Now he was a mighty man of God, working across the continent of Africa to bring the light that pierces the darkness which, as he knew only too well, really exists.

Darko, as he was invariably called, had to assume the role of the head of the family when he was only a child, because his father died. He was the eldest and there were four other children to care for, so he started trading. Because he was a highly intelligent boy, Darko was able to win scholarships to get an education up to secondary school level. After that, he had to stay at home because his mother could not pay the difference between the scholarship funds and the fees at the secondary school. Nothing daunted, he started a correspondence course with a college in England.

When he was 16, a friend who knew about his constant dreams suggested they should go to a miracle healing crusade being held in Kumasi. Darko didn't see what good this could do, but his friend was so persistent that he agreed. That night he heard a man preach on Psalm 91, 'He who dwells in the secret place of the most High shall abide under the shadow of the Almighty.' The preacher went on to say that there were more promises in verses 7 and 8: 'A thousand may fall at your side, and ten thousand at your right hand; but it shall not come near you. Only with your eyes shall you look and see the reward of the wicked.' There is yet more, he told them. Verse 14 says, 'Because he has set his love upon me, therefore I will deliver him; I will set him on high, because he has known my name.' The power with which those words came to Darko challenged him. Even though he had heard the word of God in the mission school, never had it come with such power. He was the first out for salvation when the preacher gave the call to come forward. Darko told them how he couldn't sleep because of the evil spirits taunting him and so they prayed, rebuking the demonic oppression in the name of Jesus.

When he got ready for bed that night, Darko quoted John 1:12 and 13, just as the preacher had told him to, and then added, 'I am Your child, God, and I am going to sleep tonight. Take care of me.' So excited was he the following morning, having slept soundly, that he rushed round to tell the preacher about it. Shortly afterwards, Darko was baptized in the Holy Spirit and the word of God became so real to him that he read the whole Bible within a few weeks. In his words, 'I was a fast reader and I read day and night.' God had given him a gift, and he started memorizing the word. When people speak to Darko the Scriptures just pour out of him, they became such an integral part of the man.

Darko heard that Israel was offering scholarships, so he went along for an interview and they told him he was just the sort of guy they were looking for. At the age of 17 he went to study, on a government scholarship, at Ruppin Institute in Israel, and four years later came home with a diploma in agricultural science and poultry husbandry.

The year he returned from Israel, his mother remarried. Her new husband was a lecturer at the university. He had become interested in the work Darko was doing with the government on farming poultry and decided to set up a poultry farm. Darko resigned from his government job and worked with his stepfather. Within six years they were prospering, but his stepfather did not know the Lord and the money being made for him by his stepson was spent without any thought. Darko began praying: he could see a parallel between his situation and that of Jacob.

After six years, the situation was brought to a head in a way that was most unexpected. Maurice Cerullo came to Kumasi and Darko, as a youth leader in his church, was one of the people assigned to be a counsellor for the crusade. He went to his stepfather to ask him for two weeks off work. Throughout the entire time he had worked for his stepfather, Darko had not taken any holidays, but to his amazement his stepfather refused to give him even a day off. Darko had to make a decision as to whether or not he should defy this man. He stood before his stepfather and said, 'It is my right to have leave for the six years I have worked for you. I cannot allow this to stand between me and God and so, whether you like it or not, I am going.' His stepfather fired him and told him not to come back. So Darko went.

The crusade began. The first week was spent in prayer and fasting; for the second week, Darko was acting as a chauffeur and interpreter. He noticed that most of the pastors who came were wearing shirts discoloured by age and big coats given to them by American missionaries. He thought to himself that it was wrong for people who were God's ministers to be wearing tatty clothes. He spoke to Maurice Cerullo about the pastors and how he wanted to start his own business so that he could support them. The reply was that God had given Darko a ministerial gift of help. 'If you have the desire to give money in this way, then it is the Lord talking to you. This is a great gift that the Lord has put in your spirit,' Cerullo prayed over him.

When his stepfather had sacked him, Darko's original intention had been to go to Bible School, but God spoke clearly to him, saying that He wanted him to be a business man and support His work. That year Darko married Christina, then working at the government hospital in Kumasi as a nursing officer. Soon afterwards, his stepfather asked him to come back, with the agreement that he would work his own farm on a part-time basis. He gave Darko 1,000 cedis as well (at that time, one cedi equalled one US dollar). With that and his savings of 1,000 cedis, Darko acquired a 5-acre plot on a 50-year lease and started a 900-bird egg farm. Knowing the word of God as he did, Darko knew the importance of tithing. He read again Malachi 3:8–10, in which it says, 'Will a man rob God? Yet you have robbed me! ... in tithes and offerings ... Bring all the tithes into the storehouse ... see if I will not open for you the windows of heaven.' He had already paid his tithes, but to show God how much he took Him at His word, Darko paid another tithe on top. It was a lot of money, but he was proving God.

About a year later, he realized they needed more money and would need a loan from the bank. The problem was, he had no collateral, but he believed the Scriptures about the man in the Gospels who, because he was persistent, had the door opened to him. Darko made his appointment and explained his plight to the managing director. He trusted Darko and said he was happy to take the leasehold as his collateral. He lent him 5,000 cedis for one year. Within six months, Darko had repaid the loan from his profits, with the result that the director trusted him even more. 'We like doing business with you and would be willing to lend you more money to expand your farm.' After leaving his stepfather's business entirely, he borrowed one million cedis that God enabled him easily to repay.

His business was now very prosperous, and one day the Lord reminded him about the pastors and the shirts. In London for a church conference, Darko bought a thousand shirts of varying sizes and shipped them back to Ghana. When he returned to Africa, he called a meeting at which there were about 300 pastors. He shared the story of his vow to God, and told them they could each choose three shirts. Everyone in the meeting was in tears.

In 1980 Darko heard about the Full Gospel Business Men's Fellowship International. Instantly, he realized that this was a vehicle to touch the business people, and opened a chapter in Kumasi. When Don Ostrom, from Seattle chapter, went over three years later and saw what Darko was achieving, he told him: 'I have seen the Spirit of God in you. You are a generous man.' Darko said that this was not so, he just had the gift of helps. But increasingly he gave away, buying breakfasts and lunches for people and travelling for the FGBMFI. In 1984, when he shared his testimony at the world convention, Demos said, 'I see the Holy Spirit in you and I love you because I can see the glow in you.'

Fired up more than ever and armed with lots of materials from America, Darko moved every week from city to city, opening new chapters. He had lots of Christian contacts through Scripture Union and he used these in the various places. In three years he opened sixty chapters, with hundreds of members. He then started travelling across the continent to Sierra Leone, Liberia and Kenya, and then in 1987 went to the European convention in Grenoble, France. While

there, Darko met a diplomat for Togo, at that time representing his country in Canada. This diplomat had learned about
FGBMFI when he was in a hotel in Canada and had seen on
the television that there was to be a meeting in his hotel. He
had been so excited to learn about the European convention in
Grenoble and, Togo being French-speaking, he had wanted to
go. As soon as Darko met him the Lord spoke to his heart and
told him to go and open up Togo for the Fellowship. Darko
and Christina travelled to Togo and, with his Scripture Union
contacts, organized a meeting and shared the vision with
them. Darko paid for a hundred breakfasts for the first chapter, and the work was then established in that country.

A Pan-African Council was set up, headed by Darko. In
1991 he travelled outside Ghana more than fifty times for the
Fellowship. Every week he was in a different town or city, and
he spent around $70,000 of his own money – except he says
that it's the Lord's money, because God has given him the
ability to make it through business. By 1993 he had opened
chapters in 40 countries in Africa, a long way from that dark
tunnel of his childhood. Darko continued to work and travel, encouraging and helping the FGBMFI, believing in his
heart that when God told him not to go to Bible School but
into business, this was what He had in mind. He summed it
up by saying, 'I am just an instrument for the Lord.'

Occult practices were very prevalent in Africa. Akin
Famodimu experienced the death of his mother when only a
young child and grew up under a lot of oppression by the
powers of darkness. Then his father died in a suspicious
motor vehicle accident. Both parents had been Christians.
His paternal grandfather, however, had 'African' powers
to heal people, especially those with mental disorders. It was
then believed in Nigeria that mystical power came from
India, and Akin determined to go to that country to fortify
himself against evil forces.

A university degree and a good job in marketing with Lever Brothers did not bring happiness. Akin's wife suffered many miscarriages. In Africa, at times like that, it was the practice for relatives to take a couple to 'prayer houses'. These were 'fetish churches', with nothing at all relating to Christianity. Neither Akin nor his wife wanted to go, but felt they had no option. Akin knew the Bible from his Christian upbringing but had never experienced Jesus in a real way. Then an old friend came and talked to them about God. She had committed her life to Jesus, and she was so persistent that eventually they came to realize this was the truth and asked Jesus to come into their lives in the same way.

Akin travelled regularly to the United States, attending Christian seminars at a Bible College, and on one of these trips he met Sam Mbata, an International Director for the FGBMFI in Nigeria. He told Akin about the organization, but it was not until a lady invited him to the world convention in Melbourne, Australia, that he came fully to learn about the Fellowship. As he checked out of the Sheraton Hotel, an Australian came up and refunded all his hotel costs. At that, Akin broke down as the realization dawned on him of how much God cared. That gift enabled him to buy all the audio and video tapes from the convention! Akin founded the first Lagos chapter. Since then, the Fellowship in Nigeria has grown phenomenally. They now have nearly 900 chapters and over 10,000 members.

In Togo, until the Fellowship made a breakthrough the country remained closed to the Pentecostal movement. Following the first FGBMFI convention in that country, they attracted important national leaders, including members of their Cabinet, who accepted the Lord and were active members of the Fellowship. Huge publicity was allowed on television and the radio for the convention meetings. It was a great opening.

Gratien de Souza was the national president of Togo, not a man to be overlooked. He stood at over six and a half feet tall. Before he became a Christian, Gratien was very ill – in fact he was dying. His family did everything for him, including taking him to the ju-ju man. He expected the ju-ju man to work his magic, but nothing improved his situation. Gratien's cousin was a member of the FGBMFI and was always asking him to go to the meetings, but Gratien thought they only wanted his money. He was a very successful business man. The family put a lot of pressure on him to see the ju-ju man again, but eventually his cousin persuaded him to go and meet Allan Jones from England. After they talked, Allan and the other men prayed for Gratien, and he felt as if fire was going through him. God released him from all the evil powers that had oppressed him and caused the illness. He accepted Jesus as his Saviour and his face radiated with joy as he sought to serve the Lord Jesus.

Victor Adossi was another FGBMFI leader in Togo. One day, he had to sack one of his workers, which resulted in Victor being questioned by the labour administrator about his reasons for dismissing the man. Suddenly she said to Victor, 'Are you born again?' He tried to evade answering directly, but eventually had to admit he was not. This woman invited him to an FGBMFI meeting. The first time he went and saw the people dancing and enjoying themselves, he said there was no way he could do anything like that. When the call for salvation was given he would not go forward for prayer. However, the woman asked him again, and at the next meeting Victor was just waiting for the speaker to ask for those people who wanted to become Christians to go to the front. He was the first there! Since that time he has seen God enable him to open his own company, and to travel both with his job and for the Fellowship. On one occasion, in Ghana, his car suddenly stopped and he realized he had forgotten to fill it up. With some way to go to a petrol station, Victor was more than a little concerned. Then he just put his hand on the tank and said, 'Fill it in the name of Jesus until I get to the next petrol station.' He got back into the car, and it started immediately; as he pulled up at the next filling station, the car stopped.

In Central Africa, consisting of eleven countries including Burundi, Rwanda and Zaire, there were 1,258 chapters and over 32,000 members. Despite all the political problems, the civil wars and food shortages, God was blessing these nations spiritually. When the 1999 world convention took place in Anaheim, many members from these countries were unable to attend because, they were told, had they travelled to the USA they would not have been allowed back home.

The Bellevue, Washington, chapter of FGBMFI, under the leadership of Roger Sonnesyn, had been travelling to Uganda and Rwanda each year for four years. In Rwanda, over 500,000 people were slaughtered in a genocidal attempt to eliminate an entire tribe of people. The country was devastated by evidence that some church officials were involved in the genocide. Roger said that the reason for the fast growth in the FGBMFI chapters was that they offered a welcome relief from church politics and tribal feuds. The business and professional community of Rwanda was experiencing a powerful anointing of the Spirit of God in chapter meetings that brought refreshment from the daily suffering. This was also bringing about a healing of broken relationships. In Uganda and Rwanda, the team visited prisons and orphanages as well as churches and, of course, FGBMFI meetings. In one prison they spoke to 1,200 prisoners and estimated that around 800 raised their hand for salvation; another 600 were prayed with for healing. They believed that over the time they spent in the two countries, hundreds gave their lives to Jesus, many hundreds were baptized in the Holy Spirit and over a thousand received prayer for healing. A number of orphans were also sponsored by the Americans.

It was not easy for the Christians in these countries. Many chapter leaders in particular went through very difficult times, some undergoing ferocious personal attacks. Despite all this, they were moving forward in God's work. In 1998, a new FGBMFI chapter was opened at the famous Entebbe International Airport.

Some years previously in Gabon, the president of that country closed the doors to FGBMFI out of concern that they were becoming too powerful. Kwabeno Darko and several other Africans approached the president, telling him that if he would open Gabon to Full Gospel they would bring top men from all over Africa and the country would be blessed because of their presence. The president graciously agreed. Seventeen nations were able to come together in that tiny nation. On the Friday evening, one of the army generals was talking after the meeting with Richard Shakarian, who had flown out especially for the convention. Richard invited him back the next morning, when he would be speaking at the breakfast meeting. The Lord poured out His Spirit at the meeting, and many were healed and came forward to give testimony of the healing that had occurred. When the invitation to receive Jesus was given, the first one to respond was the army general.

Elie and Denise Yapoudijian, from France, travelled to Lubumbashi in Zaire as part of an airlift team. On their arrival, various civil leaders of Katanga province and the city of Lubumbashi, including the vice governor, mayor and burgomaster, welcomed them, and the officials were given a copy of *The Happiest People on Earth*. To their surprise, one of the burgomaster's employees exclaimed that he knew the book well, and had in fact named his youngest child Demos Shakarian! The Alliance of the Democratic Force of

Liberation political party also asked Elie and Denise to visit them and they gave out copies of *Voice* magazine.

During the visit they were interviewed by a religious radio station reaching half a million listeners, and also by a secular television programme. In Lubumbashi, Elie and Denise spoke at twenty meetings, attendance at these ranging between 400 and 700 for each meeting. They were also able to speak at the Likasi FGBMFI convention at which the theme was 'Let the glory fall on our nation'.

Zambia was visited in 1998 by John and Charlotte Carrette; this trip, by the way, enabled them to miss the terrible storms over Guatemala caused by Hurricane Mitch. For two weeks they were able to travel and share with the men of Zambia, encouraging them in their work. They found that God had already done much preparatory work, and believed that FGBMFI would grow like a strong plant. One of the reasons for this confidence was that the men of Zambia were aiming to start a work in Namibia, Botswana and South Africa. If men were looking to take this work into other countries, it was a sure sign that they had caught the vision of how God wanted to use laymen to expand this Fellowship.

FOURTEEN

Rain … and Fire!

In the few days before Hurricane Mitch hit Honduras, Richard Shakarian and his wife Vangie spent a long weekend in that country. Kiki, the young man who heads the youth chapters in Honduras, had organized a heavy schedule; with the weather closing in, they left, as they later discovered, on the last flight out before the hurricane finally struck. What they experienced in the meetings was the spiritual equivalent of the 'natural' rain that was to be let loose. Honduras and its neighbour, Nicaragua, have between them over thirty youth chapters, and at the rally organized for the young people, 700 were present, nearly half of that number committing their lives to Jesus, and many healed and baptized in the Holy Spirit. At another meeting, this time for a church, over 19,000 saw God move in miraculous ways.

Jimmy Hughes and his wife had an open home in Honduras for young people who wanted help to get off drugs or drink, or who were violent and rebellious. They adopted them for three months to a year, and discipled them in the truth so that they were set free from their torment. The day before Hurricane Mitch hit, God spoke to Jimmy and told him to go and shop, getting as much as he possibly could. Jimmy tried to tell God, and later his wife, that it wasn't his day for shopping, but he knew when to give in. He bought ten times more than he normally did. When they woke up the following morning there was no road outside, only a river roaring past their house, and it was five days before they could get out. Jimmy and his wife were able to feed fifteen people a day, and sometimes more, from the food he had bought. That didn't surprise Jimmy at all. He knew that his God was able to do anything.

Jimmy was born in Los Angeles, and stayed there when his family moved to Guatemala. He would have nothing to do with God. After spending six years in the military, he became a professional hit man for the Mafia. In his words, 'I collected money, hurt a lot of people, and saw a lot of blood. I know what it's like to cut the throat of a man, see a man die or throw a man in the boot of a car and take him to his death.' Jimmy admits to doing many terrible things. Satan had brought so much deception into his life that he was totally gullible and manipulated by evil. At one stage, he had an $8,000 a month cocaine habit and drank half a gallon of liquor a day. The one great advantage he had was a mother and sisters who were praying for him. Eventually, he says, 'I wanted out.'

His mother, who became the pastor of a church in Guatemala, arranged for a business man from there to fly to Los Angeles to meet Jimmy. It was, to say the least, a difficult time for him. The Mafia had a contract of $30,000 out on his life, and the FBI wanted to make deals with him because of all the information he possessed. From one day to the next, he didn't know whether he was going to go to prison or die. It was at this point that John Carrette, the Executive Vice President of the Fellowship, met Jimmy at the Hyatt Hotel and began to share with him about Jesus and the FGBMFI.

Jimmy was very impressed for a number of reasons. First, John was not a 'professional' man of God; he was a business man. Second, he spoke with the authority of Jesus. John prayed and prophesied over Jimmy, who said of him, 'There was something neat about this business man. He had authority in his mouth. He had the presence of God within him. The brightness of Jesus was in his eyes. I saw Jesus in his face and he spoke with power.'[1]

In the prophetic word that John gave to him, he said, 'Jimmy, God needs you in Central America. He needs you as the soldier that you were. He needs you in His army. He calls you to ministry.' Jimmy wanted to do what God had told John, but he couldn't – there were too many things he felt he had to get sorted. However, he did allow John to pray again for him, and Jimmy felt the power of God come on him.

Through a miracle – Jimmy said it was thanks to the prayers of his mother – he was able to get out of the Mafia alive. He then did what God had told him. First, he went to Guatemala where, in his words, 'John Carrette godfathered me into the Fellowship.' It wasn't too long before Jimmy was travelling all around the world, to Japan, Jamaica, Martinique, Guadeloupe, Canada and many other places, sharing his testimony in chapter meetings and conventions. He now works out of Honduras for the Fellowship as an International Director at Large.

Jimmy's whole life became a living testimony; his enthusiasm and energy were infectious. He also knows how to use the power that Jesus has given him. One day he was driving down a street in San Pedro Sula with his friend when they saw a boy being shot – two bullets in his head and one by his heart. Jimmy said that they should stop and help, but his friend said that the authorities might accuse them of doing the killing. They could end up in jail just because they were there. Jimmy turned to him and said that if they didn't stop they could have problems with God, and he knew which he'd prefer. As he jumped out of the car and ran over, he remembered what Jesus had said in Matthew 10: 7–8 'And as you go, preach, saying, "The kingdom of heaven is at hand. Heal the sick, cleanse the lepers, raise the dead, cast out demons. Freely you have received, freely give."' So he was obedient to the word of God. He had learned that God has the responsibility to be faithful to our obedience, as only He can raise the dead, heal the sick and do all these other things.

By the time Jimmy reached the young boy, the two with the guns had run off, but another young drug addict with a big bag of glue in his hand was kicking the dead body. Jesus said to cast out the demons, and in Jimmy's eyes that's exactly what this drug addict was at that moment. He grabbed him and threw him into the air and out of the way. He then knelt down and prayed three times, in the name of Jesus, 'The kingdom of heaven has come to you', praying it in English and Spanish. Jimmy knew of no formulas for raising the dead; he just had so much compassion for the boy's family. Then the boy breathed and moved, and he began to repeat what Jimmy had been saying, 'Jesus, Jesus, Jesus'. Not knowing what the outcome might be, Jimmy led him in a sinner's prayer.

Two months later, Jimmy went to look for the boy in the hospital. He was alive and well. They had taken the bullets out of his head and body. Jimmy told him who he was and how he had brought him to the hospital. The young boy began to cry like a baby and thanked Jimmy. He said that on the day he was attacked he had not known Jesus. The people who shot him wanted to take his money. All he remembered was waking up in a very dark place. It was Hell, and God did not exist there. (That blew Jimmy's mind!) The boy said he had been so afraid about being in Hell; then he heard the name of Jesus, and he woke up and heard Jimmy saying, 'Jesus, Jesus', and life came back into him.

Jimmy's testimony was that none of this would have happened without a praying mother and the Full Gospel Business Men's Fellowship International, where he learned to be an effective witness for Jesus.

'Who wants to be a millionaire?' asks the song. Rudy Rivera's answer would have been, 'I do.' He had been granted a 'special status' sometimes accorded to people who wanted to leave a Communist country and go to the USA. Consequently, he received a first-class education at a top school, even though he came from a very poor family. Determined to be a millionaire by the age of 30, he realized when he reached 25 that unless he did something very quickly, he was not going to achieve his ambition. With this in mind, he returned home to Honduras where, like King Midas, everything he touched turned to gold.

Sitting in a hotel with friends one evening, enjoying a few drinks, someone passed a remark about how much money Rudy was spending. He bragged that he deserved to enjoy it; he'd earned it. If, later, he could have retracted his next words, he would have done. 'Even if I lost it, I could do it again. Good health and hard work – that's all there is to it.'[2] Immediately, it seemed everybody was conspiring not to pay him or even buy his products. It was God's way of letting Rudy see just how much, or little, he could do on his own. The banks cut off funds. He was building a hospital when the government stopped paying. As his pride drained away, someone invited him to an FGBMFI dinner meeting, which seemed to him a good idea, in his state.

Two Americans from New York State talked about how God had made a difference in their lives. They talked about marriage problems and collapsing businesses they had experienced, and yet now they were successful. Their stories touched Rudy because they spoke about his situation. Having lost all hope, he needed God. Ironically, his financial situation was so bad he couldn't even pay for his American-born wife to get an airline ticket home when she wanted to leave him!

'God's got something for you,' they said. Rudy had always thought that everything could be solved by money, but he knew they weren't talking about that. 'What have you done for God?' A strange question, thought Rudy. He'd attended church and been involved with various activities there; what else could he say? 'I go to church every Sunday,' Rudy replied. One of the men smiled. 'Putting a horse in the garage doesn't make it into a car.' They led Rudy in a prayer, asking that God would forgive him and fill his life. The men then told him about the Holy Spirit.

As he and his wife, Charolette, drove home, they had a conversation, most unusual as they'd come to the point where they didn't talk any more – there didn't seem anything to say. Something else strange was happening. Rudy kept speaking in a strange language. He later learned that this was the baptism of the Holy Spirit; he thought they must have hypnotized him. The following day, when he was looking for an explanation of why he felt this wonderful peace, someone explained to him, 'Rudy, you are a new creation in Christ Jesus. You have committed your life to God.' He asked what he should do next, and was told, 'Do nothing. Let Jesus take control.'[3]

Rudy was still in a terrible financial situation, so bad that they were going to cut off the electricity. He asked for one more day to pay, then pulled out the bill and prayed, asking the Lord not to leave his wife and children without electricity. Literally the moment he stopped praying, a customer came around the corner for tiles, and he had the money. Rudy and Charolette quickly learned to trust God in all aspects of their lives. Their daughter was diagnosed with a heart defect and, two years later, the doctor said she might need surgery. Having no money to pay for medical bills, they got together with their friends and prayed in agreement that God would heal her. The following week the doctor could find no sign of any defect. Rudy told the doctor they had been praying, and he agreed it was a miracle. She was to go on to become the best athlete in the school and the national champion in tennis for her age.

In the year before the hurricane, Rudy Rivera travelled a number of times to the UK, believing that God had told him to encourage the chapters. On one occasion, he brought with him a number of other men: Jaime Sol from El Salvador, John Allard who runs a work feeding children in Honduras, and Jorge Auil from Belize. All the men shared testimony in a number of chapters and churches around the country and were a blessing to everyone who met and heard them.

One of the directors in Honduras, Jose Adrian Velasquez, was known as 'the rice king'. Jose was a very prosperous business man with a number of companies, and a man who loved God with all his heart. One day as he was praying, the Lord spoke to him: 'Jose, what about your customers?' Puzzled, Jose's response was, 'What about my customers, God?' He had no idea what God was talking about – he had never come across the word 'customer' in the New Testament. God asked him the question again, and received the same answer from Jose. Then God made this somewhat chilling statement: 'I gave them to you that they would bless you and I gave them to you so that you could bring them to me. When you stand in front of me I will ask you about them.' Jose thought he'd better move into action.

For some time he prayed about what he should do, and it came to him that he should have a big dinner and invite all his customers along. Invitations were sent out for a banquet with a nationally known singer who would be singing love songs. Few people can resist a free meal, especially one which they know will be of a high quality. Eight hundred people came and sat down to a superb banquet, and the singer, as promised, sang some well-known love songs. Then he began to sing a love song to Jesus, and followed it with a personal testimony of how he had turned his life over to Jesus. When he had finished, Jose stood up and said, 'The reason we asked you here was to tell you about our friend, the Lord Jesus Christ, to give you a chance of making him your friend as well. If you would like to accept Jesus into your life in the way the singer and I have done, then I invite you to get to your feet.' Every one of the 800 people stood!

It caught on. One of the leading politicians asked Jose if he would do the same thing in his house – it was a very large mansion. Jose did exactly what he had done before. Within twelve months he had invited 150,000 people to dinners, and around two-thirds of them had accepted Jesus as Saviour.

Jorge Auil had first heard about the Fellowship many years previously. He was deputy manager at Barclays Bank International, Belize City branch, married with five children, and suggests 'Catholic pagan' is close when describing his religious state. Along the road to a successful life, Jorge had become an alcoholic. It had started at the age of 17 and continued throughout his married life. Looking back, he was amazed at how he made progress in the bank given that his personal and family life was such a shambles. Rather like Rudy, Jorge said the only reason his wife did not leave him was because she didn't have the money for the airfare and was too proud to ask her mother!

A friend came into the bank one day and invited him to go on a weekend trip to Caye Chapel, which was one of a number of small islands dotting the reef along the coast of Belize. People went there for recreation, swimming and scuba-diving. Jorge accepted the invitation without any hesitation, thinking it would be another 'lost weekend' with friends, carousing and maybe even doing a little fishing. 'Good,' said his friend, 'I'll put your name down on the list.' He then told Jorge a little more about the weekend: how it was planned for prominent men in the public and private sector. There would be a group of business men from Houston, called the Full Gospel Business Men's Fellowship International, who were sponsoring the trip, and they would all be staying at a brand new hotel.

Hearing that a religious group were to be involved, Jorge immediately retracted his acceptance. He had long strayed away from the Lord, and while he still believed there was a God and a hereafter, they seemed very distant and not particularly relevant to his everyday life. Jorge always figured there would be time for repentance later. He also considered himself something of a he-man and thought Christians were a bunch of sissies. 'Thank God,' Jorge said, 'my friend persisted.' Telling him that there would be lawyers, doctors, entrepreneurs of various kinds and even a couple of millionaires who would be flying down in their own planes – that's what did it. The desire to meet the millionaires, and perhaps get some new business for the bank, swung the balance.

Jorge organized himself for the trip, checking his toiletries and a few items of personal clothing in the overnight bag. Then, at the last minute, he thought he'd better put in something else – a bottle of Johnny Walker Black Label Whisky, in case he needed a drink after the hotel bar closed!

He wasn't sure what to expect. Everyone seemed to get along extremely well, despite all the different denominations. In fact, they were friendly to the point that he found their laughter, hugging and expressions of love a bit revolting. But this camaraderie continued the following day, and after hearing some of their testimonies, Jorge began secretly to want to be like them. When the Saturday night speaker challenged them to accept Jesus into their lives, there was a war going on inside him. Jorge wanted to have Jesus transform his life, but at the same time there was another voice telling him not to be a fool. How could he give control of his life to someone else, even if that someone else was God?

The battle was eventually won, in God's favour, and Jorge was able to step forward and receive the life-transforming love and forgiveness he desperately needed. What a difference that made in his life, the life of his family and his business. Jorge was actively involved in FGBMFI in Belize after that weekend, seeing men with lives very similar to his, working in their churches, or helping the poor and disadvantaged, or involved in prison ministries. The revival which spread throughout Central America in 1999 brought growth in the number of chapters and the membership.

The *Guinness Book of Records* describes him as the 'World's Most Successful Advocate', having never lost a case in 232 murder trials: Sir Lionel Luckhoo, KCMG, CBE, QC, has had a distinguished career in many fields. He was once a member of the executive council of Georgetown, Guyana, and served four times as its mayor. He is the owner, with his brother, of over a hundred racehorses, is a former president of the Guyana Olympic Association, and had the unique distinction of representing the two independent countries of Guyana and Barbados as High Commissioner and Ambassador accredited to London, Paris, Bonn and The Hague. He was the only man ever to represent two countries simultaneously and, as such, receive two degrees of knighthood from the Queen.

Sir Lionel received an invitation to a Full Gospel Business Men's Fellowship International dinner in the Pegasus Hotel, Georgetown, in November 1978.[4] Immediately he was put off by the long name, by the fact that it was religious, and because it was 'Yankee'. He decided they could well manage without his presence. About three hours before the dinner, however, he received a phone call asking if he was planning to attend. Having intended to say a definite 'no', he found himself accepting. 'Quietly religious' summed up his assessment of himself. He rarely read the Bible, but believed there was God. Assured by the men from America that this was not a cult and that the only purpose of the Fellowship was to 'lift up Jesus' through its world-wide organization of chapters, he was not impressed, and thought them idealistic and not very practical. Listening to the testimonies did bring a response, however. These people had experienced a new dimension of life, unlike anything he'd known, and the peace and joy that came through had always eluded him.

When the people were asked to indicate that they wanted to know more about Jesus, he looked around, debating inside whether he should respond. He said, 'It seemed as though Jesus was knocking at the door of my heart, bidding me open to Him. I stood and accepted Jesus by faith. That was the beginning of a complete change, a total transformation of my life. I was born again.'[5]

One week after the dinner, the tragic suicide/mass murder of more than 900 people took place in Jonestown, Guyana. Sir Lionel had been attorney for Jim Jones, the leader of the group, and had narrowly escaped death on the day when US Congressman Leo Ryan and others flew to meet Jones. As the people alighted from the plane, they were shot dead. Sir Lionel had not accompanied them: something inside, that he later realized was the Holy Spirit, kept telling him not to go.

The day before the tragedy in Jonestown, a letter had gone to the prime minister of Guyana, inviting him and other dignitaries to a special dinner hosted by the FGBMFI. Convinced that he would not accept the invitation in view of all the bad publicity surrounding the country, the Fellowship were delighted when he agreed to attend. It was a resounding success. The prime minister told Sir Lionel how impressed he was with the group of business men, and they saw many people accepting Jesus and being baptized in the Holy Spirit. Always wanting the evidence to be recorded, Sir Lionel noted that 47 people claimed to have been healed, including a deaf and dumb man whose ears were opened and who left the platform saying his first words: 'I love God. I love God.'

Sir Lionel became a great ambassador for the FGBMFI, travelling to many countries all over the world to speak at conventions and chapter meetings. He claims to have covered nearly a million miles to preach the Gospel. As he so eloquently puts it, 'It is the greatest case I have ever pleaded and I am confident, because all the evidence is on our side. The verdict must be that Jesus Christ is Lord, and that He is coming back soon to proclaim His people "not guilty" and to take us to be with Him forever.'[6]

John Carrette first came in touch with the Fellowship way back in 1978. He was in Los Angeles, watching television, flicking through the channels, when he saw Demos Shakarian, who was saying, 'We are celebrating the 1978 world convention in Anaheim. Tomorrow night is our last meeting and Oral Roberts is the speaker, so come on down!' John had been a Christian for ten years and his desire to serve the Lord had grown in that time, but he had not yet found his particular direction. He knew he did not want to be in full-time ministry in the sense of being a pastor; rather, he wanted to serve the Lord as a business man.

The following night, along with his father-in-law, John went to the Convention Centre. The place was packed with around 15,000 people, and the two men were sent up the third balcony, where the only available seats were the last ones against the wall. Oral Roberts preached his now famous sermon on 'the Fourth Man'. (Every time people heard this it had the effect of almost lifting them off their feet!) The first call Oral made that night was for salvation, and John watched as about a thousand went forward. When Oral had finished, Demos came out to close the convention, then paused and said, 'The Lord is telling me to make one more call. If you are here tonight and you want to serve the Lord, come down here to the front.' John had never heard this kind of call given, but knew it was for him. He stood to his feet and immediately the Devil whispered in his ear that he would be the only one, in front of 15,000 people. Such a desire was there inside him that John ignored the voice, got to his feet and started to walk down. When he got to the second balcony, 25 men joined him, and at the next balcony, 100 men. No one said a word – total silence. By the time the group reached the front of the Convention Centre there were about 300 men. It was at this same convention that Blair Scott made his commitment to serve the Lord.

John and his wife Charlotte ran a hotel in Guatemala. When he returned home, he talked to a pastor and told him of the desire to bring men together into his hotel for a meeting. John spent that first meeting making pancakes in the hotel kitchens! It was the start of FGBMFI in Guatemala. Some men from Honduras and Seattle came over and, with Fred Ladenius as the main speaker, they held their first dinner and then set up chapters. All of this happened within six months.

Prior to this, John had heard of the FGBMFI but had not wanted to go. He felt that if he went, one of their people would be able to read the sins in his life just by looking at him. The Fellowship had such a reputation for power. Now, such was John's desire to serve God, he wanted that power working through him. Talking of the hunger men have to be used of God, John said that the job of the FGBMFI is to turn men into soul-winners. 'We are anointed for that purpose. Think of the Fellowship as a kind of seminary to produce laymen for ministry. If we don't do that then the anointing is not on us.'

Florencio De Leon's story has to be one the greatest testimonies to the power of God. To say he was born disadvantaged is the biggest understatement. Florencio was born and
lived on a rubbish dump. He was fortunate to be alive. His
food source was the bins, and he was totally destitute and
filthy. One day he was standing on a street in Guatemala
City outside the biggest hotel. Two men who were smartly
dressed in suits asked him if he would like to go in to a lunch
that was taking place: they would pay for him. He looked at
the business men and how they were dressed, and looked
down at himself, dirty and in rags. Then he looked at the big
hotel and said he couldn't go in there.

'Why not?' they replied. 'We're inviting you.'

Florencio said, 'I have no shoes.'

No problem. 'Forget about your shoes, just come in with
us,' they replied. It was a chapter meeting, a very high-
class affair, with men from the American Embassy and the
World Bank and many other business men, and they seated
Florencio next to an architect. He ate a fantastic lunch and
then listened to a story of how Jesus had changed someone's
life, and then about the Shakarian family, when Demos had
prayed for his cows to be healed in the name of Jesus and they
were. At the close of the luncheon, Florencio prayed, 'O
God, if you can heal Demos' cows, perhaps you could change
me.' That day he committed his life to Jesus, was filled with
the Holy Spirit and his life was transformed. He learned the
reality of Romans 8:31, 'If God is for us, who can be against
us?' He could have died from disease, or malnutrition, or
been killed – *but* God was for him. Florencio travelled to
fourteen different countries sharing his story and became a
leader in the FGBMFI.

'God,' prayed Demos Shakarian, 'when are you going to
move and bring multitudes of souls into the kingdom before
the return of Jesus Christ? Too many people are dying and

going to hell without ever hearing the name of Jesus.' The answer from God surprised Demos. 'I'm waiting on you. I've given you My Son, His name and His authority. I cannot give you any more. Take what I've given you, and as you go the revival you've been waiting for will break out around you.' That was in 1984, and so great a revelation was this in the eyes of Demos that he called the leaders from around the world to come to a gathering at the Lake of the Ozarks in the USA to share with them. Later he wrote about this in *The Vision Intensified*.

Sometimes it takes a while for what God has said to take root in the hearts of His people. Over those last few years, God had certainly 'stepped up the pace' in terms of the number of countries to which the Fellowship had spread, and the anointing on men, too, was growing. Richard Shakarian had been exercised in his spirit for the members of FGBMFI to move up a level in their service for the Lord, and to that end he called the leaders of the Latin American countries together to a meeting in Miami in January 1999. He told these leaders that he felt Nicaragua would be the place for God to move in a special way, to show members how to be more effective in their ministry. Agreement was unanimous, and they returned home to start planning an outreach for the first weekend of May. During their first meeting in Nicaragua, they heard that one of the members had had a vision where he saw wheat fields, ready for harvesting. When the men turned to John 4:35–8, they discovered that Jesus had said: 'Do you not say, "There are still four months and then comes the harvest?" Behold, I say to you, lift up your eyes and look at the fields for they are already white for harvest.' It was four months from their meeting to the planned outreach!

The strategy which they believed the Lord gave them was to match up teachers with schools, engineers with factories, doctors with hospitals, soldiers with bases, and so on. This outreach was not to be chapter meetings in a hotel or restaurant, but going out to the people, where they were. Without any difficulties, the doors began to open. In some factories, employers said they would let their workers finish 30 minutes early to hear what the men had to say!

A police commander, who was a former Catholic Sandinista, went to John Carrette and asked forgiveness of him because he had secretly hated John, a 'green beret' man, seeing him as a representative of American Protestants. They knelt together in prayer as tears flowed down their faces. The commander joined the Fellowship and arranged for his police station to have a visit from the FGBMFI men to share their testimonies.

Men and women were encouraged to come from around the world and form 'fire teams', small groups to go out and give testimony of God's powerful love in their lives and then to minister in the power of the Holy Spirit. Initially over 400 meetings were planned, but God had greater things in mind. By the end of the five days, 925 meetings had been held in every conceivable venue, some with just a handful of people, others with hundreds present.

From the national newspapers to television, the outreach was a major topic of the news, bringing a positive message of hope to a country that had had more than its share of challenges. One headline read, 'A World Leader Comes to Nicaragua'. The people were wide open to receive FGBMFI International President Richard Shakarian, representing the 145 nations in which the Fellowship is active. There had been several prophetic words concerning this event, indicating the country and the timing. Richard had to delay his planned departure by two days through the civil strife which had closed the airport. The timing of the outreach turned out to be right. A week earlier would have been impossible, but by the time the teams arrived from the USA, Central and South

America and other parts of the world, the people were looking for a miracle.

Sr Arnoldo Aleman, president of Nicaragua, graciously received the FGBMFI men, as did the opposition leader, Daniel Ortega. Both these key men were prayed for, as was the nation. Richard prayed for the country on the most popular secular TV interview show, and there were so many invitations for teams to speak that it was impossible to get to all of them.

Imagine a police station with all the young cadets, and other officers sitting in a room, waiting for men to come and share their testimony. This happened during the outreach. At the allotted time, no one turned up and so they phoned the fire team headquarters to see what had happened. Members were quickly praying as they listened to the police chief asking where their representatives were. As they were about to say they didn't know, a Christian policeman walked in through the door. 'He's on his way,' they said.

Youth teams went to schools, colleges and universities to share their testimonies and the good news about Jesus with the students. They were received with great enthusiasm and openness. This group alone counted 24,353 young people who invited Jesus into their lives during the meetings. Pupils and teachers were coming to the team, asking such questions as 'What is happening here? That boy who is crying on the floor is the worst in the school!' Not any more. God had touched him, and many more of similar ilk.

In total, over 97,000 people acknowledged that they wanted to know more about Jesus during those five days! It was a mobilization of ordinary people, each one armed with a single confidence: 'God can do it.' Whatever the need, 'God can do it.' They had been trained to give short testimonies, and went in the power of the Holy Spirit. No one could have anticipated the results in Nicaragua – it was all of God.

Jaime Sol from El Salvador reported that it was like being at a train station. There was so much happening that it was like catching a train. Every few minutes one was going somewhere new – it was only a matter of getting on board! The group from his nation went back on fire with excitement about what God had done. They had seen the blind see and the lame walk, but, more importantly, they had seen how God could use them to reach people for Jesus. In June, the city of San Miguel on the southern coast of El Salvador held a convention following the pattern used in Nicaragua. Fifty meetings were set up, and the fire came. The same excitement was felt as the men prepared for great numbers of new believers. This was what Demos Shakarian saw in the spirit: ordinary men and women bringing multitudes into the Kingdom by the power of the Holy Spirit. It continued to spread into Panama, Colombia, Belize – and from there? We wait and see.

FIFTEEN

Men from over the Mountain

The Prophetic Word

What should they take with them? Only those possessions the family could carry on their back, he decided; the rest must be sold for whatever money they could get. In his own load he would carry the heavy wood-burning brass samovar, a tangible link with the old way of life. The farm had been sold, their papers were in order, it was time to go.

For the Shakarian family of Kara Kala in Armenia, 1905 was the year of their 'exodus'. Five years had passed since the first of their friends and neighbours had left for the United States, and now Grandfather Demos was to follow in their footsteps. The journey would be long, expensive and more than a little difficult, with a wife, six daughters, a 13-year-old son and their remaining worldly possessions. Such decisions were not undertaken lightly. Tragic events had caused families like the Shakarians to take this monumental step.

Armenians were an Indo-European people with a highly distinctive culture. They embraced Christianity late in the third century. Their native land was absorbed into north eastern Turkey and what was the old USSR. (On September 9 1991, Armenians voted overwhelmingly for independence from the Soviet Union, which collapsed that December.)

As part of the Ottoman Empire until 1918, they suffered a great deal at the hands of the Turkish Moslems. In 1895–1896, over 300,000 Armenians were massacred, and in the following years nearly two million died in further massacres and forced marches.

But this Armenian family did not leave their native land because of massacre or forced march, but because of a word from God Himself. In 1900, a band of travelling Russian Christians came to Kara Kala. At one of their meetings they prayed with Grandfather Demos, laying their hands on his head. He burst into joyous prayer, not in his native tongue but in a language he had never learned. Grandfather Demos had experienced the baptism in the Holy Spirit.

Following this experience, he began to believe prophetic messages that had been given to the people of his village. One of these was particularly remarkable. About the middle of the nineteenth century, an 11-year-old boy called Efim, who had an amazing capacity for prayer, spent seven days praying and fasting. During that time, God gave him a vision in which he saw charts and a message in beautiful handwriting. He asked for pen and paper and copied every shape and diagram that came in the vision. What was extraordinary was that this boy could not then, or later, read or write. The message declared that in future days all Christians would be in danger of their lives, and that unless everyone in the region fled they would be brutally murdered. Through the maps copied by Efim, God clearly directed his people to go and settle on the west coast of the United States of America.

In 1905, God spoke again through Efim, announcing that the time had come when the vision would be fulfilled. Grandfather Demos and many others had no hesitation in acting upon God's word. They sold their possessions and set out in faith.

The early years were very hard. All the money from the sale of the farm had been used to finance their journey, and jobs were not easy to find in America. The death of Grandfather Demos only a year after their arrival left his son, Isaac, head of the family at the age of 14. Again, it was a word from God which gave direction for the future. God spoke through Deuteronomy 28: 3–8 concerning His blessings on His people and on the land. Isaac believed this word for himself, and by the time he was 20 was not only able to buy arable land and three milk cows, but also able to marry the beautiful young daughter of another Armenian family, Zarouhi Yessayian. God blessed them, and on 21 July 1913 their first child was born. They called him Demos, after his grandfather.

From the time of their arrival in California, the Armenian Pentecostals always met together on Sunday afternoons in the front room of the Shakarian home in Boston Street, Los Angeles. As their numbers grew, a small church building was constructed on Gless Street. Jesus was at the centre of their lives, and they brought up their children to know and love Him. Young Demos was no exception. He knew Jesus as a close friend from a very early age and loved to talk to Him while working in the fields.

When he was 10 years old, Demos broke his nose. It did not heal correctly, leaving the ear canal and nasal passages blocked. Eventually this resulted in acute deafness that the doctor was unable to cure in spite of several operations. But Demos harboured no resentment, only a belief that Jesus could heal him in a miraculous way.

One Sunday morning in 1926, Demos experienced a strange but pleasant feeling as he prepared for church. This was always the highlight of the week. His three younger sisters were chattering excitedly, but Demos was unable to participate because of his deafness. There was a tremendous expectancy in the air as the Armenian congregation gathered, because God had been doing wonderful things among them. As the service progressed, Demos experienced a warm sensation, as if someone was putting a heavy woollen blanket over his shoulders, but looking round he couldn't see anyone touching him. He was filled with longing to tell Jesus how much he loved Him, and, like his grandfather, began to speak in a language he did not know.

Many hours later, in his room at home, still very much aware of the Lord's presence, he heard Jesus speaking to him. Three times the Lord asked him if he would ever doubt His power, and three times Demos answered, 'No, Lord Jesus.' The next morning brought great excitement when Demos realized that for the first time in three years he could hear. Knowing his healing was for a purpose, he asked the Lord to show him the work He wanted him to do.

Over the next few years the Shakarian family prospered, eventually owning the largest dairy herd in California. Their business even flourished throughout the Depression, and they began to cherish dreams of owning the biggest herd in the world. But Demos had other dreams on his mind. By 1932, he had already chosen the woman he wished to marry. She was called Rose. Being an obedient son he followed the Armenian tradition in which the parents would meet and consult before giving their consent. This tradition also forbade any contact between the young couple until the official engagement. Demos had mentally prepared speeches over and over again, but when the time came, his first words to Rose were that he knew God wanted them together. To his amazement, she told him that she had always prayed that those would be the first words spoken to her by the man she was to marry!

Part of the prophecy given back in Kara Kala had promised that God would bless and prosper them, but there was more. God also promised that, like Abraham, he would cause their seed to be a blessing to the nations. As Demos saw the first part being fulfilled in the early years of his marriage, he began to wonder about the second. Was God asking them to do something more than just be good employers and generally helpful in the community? He began to pray regularly that once again the Lord would show him the direction he was to go.

Faithful to His word, God spoke clearly to Demos in a vision. He showed him a large park where their family often went for picnics. Many people were sitting on the grass, and in the middle was a large platform on to which he climbed and began to tell the people about Jesus. God had also given the same vision to Rose. However, one aspect of the vision troubled Demos – he found it difficult to speak out in public. But such was his faith and love for Jesus that some weeks later he found himself standing in the open air in front of a crowd, with a microphone in a somewhat clammy hand. Surely all those sermons he had listened to would enable him to speak that afternoon? Many readers will sympathize with Demos as he struggled to tell the people of his neighbourhood about Jesus. After some time, a man near the platform began to weep. He said that Demos' words were true, and that God had been very good to him as well. Taking the microphone from Demos, he began to tell the crowd his story. He was followed by someone else, and by the end of that afternoon six people had committed themselves to following Jesus.

This one meeting set the pattern not just for local evangelism but eventually for city-wide campaigns. Demos, very much aware that he was not a speaker, began to realize that God had called him to be a helper. His role was to organize these campaigns, which often lasted a number of weeks, and bring in well-known speakers. He also encouraged pastors from all denominations to work together and pray together.

At the end of the campaign, people who had made a commitment to Jesus would be shared among the denominations so that every church benefited.

It was not until many years later, during meetings in the summer of 1944, that a thought crystallized which had been in the back of his mind for a long time. As an Armenian, Demos was used to a male-dominated church. Not only were men the decision-makers in the church, but they would be present at every meeting. Over the years, however, Demos had increasingly noticed that the congregations at the meetings he organized were predominantly female. In fact, the ratio seemed to be about ten women to one man. He asked his close friend, Dr Charles Price, if all the men in the Los Angeles area were overseas. Somewhat puzzled at the question, Price replied that there had never been so many men in the area. When Demos gave the reason for his question, Price laughed at his friend's naivety, explaining to this very Armenian man that American men did not consider Christianity compatible with masculinity. In America, apart from the clergy, women were the Church.

The two friends discussed this issue many times, trying to figure out exactly why successful American business men, in particular, were rarely found inside a church. Charles confessed to Demos that when such men came to talk to him he couldn't understand their language, and their concerns were remote from his thinking. However, one statement he made was to stick in Demos' mind. It concerned the outpouring of God's blessings in the last days.

'Demos,' he said, 'I will not be here to see it, but you will witness one of the major events foretold in the Bible. Just before Jesus returns to the earth, God's Spirit is going to descend on all flesh, and laymen – ordinary men and women, people in shops and factories – will be the most important channel through whom He will work.'

Over the next seven years, Demos continued to organize meetings, the scale of these increasing. In 1951 he helped set up a series of meetings for Oral Roberts in Los Angeles. These were the biggest he had ever been involved with – approximately 200,000 people over 16 days. After the campaign, Demos explained to Oral that in spite of the obvious success of such meetings, he felt that God was calling him to something different. When Oral questioned him, Demos shared his vision for a ministry that would encourage business men to tell other business men about their experience of God. They would not preach, but simply talk in a very natural way about what God had done in their lives. He envisaged salesmen coming to listen to a man because he too was a salesman, and likewise dentists, plumbers, and so on, each speaking to men on their own level.

Demos had even settled on the name of the group: Full Gospel Business Men's Fellowship International. The title seemed a little cumbersome, but Demos explained why he had chosen it. 'Full Gospel' meant that one could share freely about everything in the Bible, whether healing, tongues or deliverance. 'Business Men' implied ordinary laymen. 'Fellowship' described a coming together of equals outside a church setting. And 'International' expressed what Demos felt God was saying about the scope of the work. Demos smiled as he explained the last word, but Oral Roberts didn't. He could see God's hand on this work.

Appendix A

Extended Extract from Prophecy through Tommy Hicks
(from the Operations Chapter Manual of FGBMFI)

As the vision appeared to me after I was asleep, I suddenly found myself in a great high distance. Where I was, I do not know. But I was looking down upon the earth. Suddenly the whole earth came into my view. Every nation, every kindred, every tongue came before my sight from the east and the west, the north and the south. I recognized every country and many cities that I had been in, and I was almost in fear and trembling as I beheld the great sight before me: and at that moment when the world came into view, it began to lightning and thunder.

As the lightning flashed over the face of the earth, my eyes went downward and I was facing the north. Suddenly I beheld what looked like a great giant, and as I stared at it, I was almost bewildered by the sight. It was so gigantic and so great. His feet seemed to reach to the north pole and his head to the south. Its arms were stretched from sea to sea. I could not even begin to understand whether this be a mountain or this be a giant, but as I watched, I suddenly beheld a great giant. I could see his head was struggling for life. He wanted to live, but his body was covered with debris from head to foot, and at times this great giant would move his body and act as though it would even raise up at times.

All of a sudden this great giant lifted his hand toward the heaven, and then it lifted its other hand, and when it did, these creatures by the thousands seemed to flee away from this giant and go into the darkness of the night.

Slowly this great giant began to rise and as he did, his head and hands went into the clouds. As he rose to his feet, he seemed to have cleansed himself from the debris and filth that was upon him, and he began to raise his hands into the heavens as though praising the Lord, and as he raised his hands, they went even unto the clouds.

(The vision goes on to describe the clouds of silver from which great drops of liquid light rained down upon the giant, and the liquid drops of light flooded the earth. The Lord Jesus Christ appeared and stretched out his hand upon the nations and the people of the world – men and women – and this liquid light flowed from his hands as a mighty anointing of God upon the people.)

… Thousands of people all over the world in Africa, England, Russia, China, America had the anointing of God upon them as they went forward in the name of the Lord. I saw these men and women as they went forth. They were ordinary people who were men and women from all walks of life. I saw people who were bound with paralysis and sickness and blindness and deafness. As the Lord stretched forth to give them this anointing, they became well, they became healed, and they went forth!

And this is the miracle of it – this is the glorious miracle of it – those people would stretch forth their hands exactly as the Lord did, and it seemed as if there was this same liquid fire in their hands. As they stretched forth their hands they said, 'According to my word, be thou made whole.'

As these people continued in this mighty end-time ministry, I did not fully realize what it was, and I looked to the Lord and asked, 'What is the meaning of this?' And he said, 'This is that, which I will do in the last days. I will restore all that the canker worm and the palmerworm, the caterpillar have destroyed (Joel 2). This, my people, in the end times will go forth. As a mighty army shall they sweep over the face of the earth.'

These people were ministering to the multitudes over the face of the earth. Tens of thousands, even millions seemed to come to the Lord Jesus Christ as these people stood forth and gave the message of the coming kingdom.

Appendix B

Father and Son, Demos and Richard Shakarian: Words of Prophecy

Demos was an incredibly humble man. To read about him, to hear him on tapes, to see him on video, is to love the man. There was something irresistible in this simple – which is not meant in any derogatory way – dairy farmer who time and again told people he was just one of God's helpers. The love of God shone out through him and was recognized by people from every walk of life. He was equally at home with the man on the street and with kings and presidents.

Returning home from a visit to Egypt where he had been to help the men set up chapters in Alexandria and Cairo and had visited the pope of the Coptic Church, he said to Rose that he thought it was time he stopped for a while and got back into the business. With that, the telephone rang and a voice said, 'The White House is calling. This is Bob Maddox. The president of the US wants you to go to Egypt.' Demos was so excited: he had never had a call from the White House before, and he asked Bob Maddox if he could ring him back in five minutes. Rose asked him if he remembered the prophecies given many years before, which had told him that he would meet world leaders. She told him to forget about staying at home, and to do what God wanted of him. He phoned Bob Maddox back and said he would be there. The next day he flew to Washington D.C., where a State Department black Cadillac was waiting for him. Demos joined the delegation that flew out from Washington, first to Egypt and then to Israel.

They met President Sadat of Egypt, and Demos gave him a copy of *The Happiest People on Earth*. The president of one of the largest life insurance companies, who was accompanying the American delegation, asked Demos if he would autograph a copy for President Carter, who had been this man's Sunday School teacher. Standing by was a US Senator, and Demos asked if he could dictate something for the Senator to write down, 'because I didn't write too well'.

A beautiful banquet was laid on by the Egyptian government for the delegation and for various leaders and officials from Egypt. While Demos was in the process of thanking the prime minister for a wonderful evening a group of men, including the Egyptian Ambassador to the United States, came across. He grabbed Demos and kissed him three times while everyone looked on, then he turned to the prime minister and said, 'I want you to know who this man is. Eighteen months ago, I was in Anaheim and they let me speak to 15,000 people at the world convention of the FGBMFI, and then I went on nationwide television. These are our friends.' The prime minister then kissed Demos, and the leading generals of Egypt followed suit.

From Egypt they flew to Sinai where about 3,000 people, including leaders of nations from around the world, were present to witness the historic transfer of land back to Egypt. With about fifteen of the American delegation, Demos walked into the huge tent that had been erected, and found that he had been placed to sit next to the pope of the Coptic Church, a beautiful and impressive-looking man with a long flowing beard. As Demos walked in, the Coptic pope stood and said, 'Mr Shakarian!' He then threw his arms around Demos, as did Bishop Samuel who was with him, while the rest of the delegation looked on in amazement. The previous evening it had been the ambassador, prime minister and leading generals – now it was the foremost Christian figure in Egypt. They were beginning to wonder who on earth this Demos Shakarian was!

Sitting in the tent looking at Mount Sinai, with all the celebrations taking place, Demos thought back to Old Testament times, with Moses at the burning bush, getting his orders from God and bringing about the release of the Children of Israel. His mind turned to Mount Ararat in Armenia, from where his family had come, and how the Russians had obeyed God's orders to go and tell the people about receiving the Holy Spirit. This had resulted in the prophecy that led not only his own family but many Armenians to safety in America. Demos thought about many of the times in his own life when God had moved mountains to enable him to rise up and go forward to do the work to which God had called him. Time and again, it was a prophetic word, spoken into the situation, which released the blessings of salvation, health and finance.

In 1993, God took Demos home to be with Him, just two days after his eightieth birthday. The funeral was a great celebration of his life, and testimony after testimony was given as to the many ways in which Demos had blessed others. Oral Roberts preached at the graveside service, and the following is a short part of his oration:

The man whose body we are committing back to earth, his spirit is speaking to us. He that is dead yet speaketh, the Bible says. He is blessed, and that blessing is a covering over his family. This dear one who died in the Lord is now resting from his labours. And it must be a great rest, for the labours were great. That is the message to us, that our rest depends upon our labours. They shall rest from their labours and their works do follow them. There is no way that Satan can interrupt Demos Shakarian's works. Hundreds of thousands of men in the business and professional world have been won to Christ, are being won to Christ, will be won to Christ in the days ahead, if Christ tarries.

Before he died, Demos put everything in order ... he had passed the mantle to his son, Richard, the new president of Full Gospel Business Men's Fellowship International. I want you to know, Richard, I affirmed your father, Demos, as the president and leader of this Fellowship, the finest group of business men this world has ever known. And with the installation of the second president of Full Gospel Business Men's Fellowship International, Richard Shakarian, the older son of Demos and Rose, the work of Full Gospel will continue unabated and with new strength and anointing. The founder and leader has finally joined with the Creator of us all, and they have talked it over, and I know that the answer is, 'Go forth.'

As a minister of the gospel, and a very close friend of Demos Shakarian for 42 years, and dear Rose, Richard, Stephen and Geri and their spouses, their children and grandchildren and all of the family and loved ones, I take these flowers and lift them to God and I want to pronounce earth to earth, dust to dust, and ashes to ashes only to the outer garment that has been worn 80 years and two days upon this earth, and is now left behind to await the day of days, and the resurrection power shall sweep in unabated …

Blessed be the Lord upon you, Richard, and on your new responsibilities, to move forward with those glorious men of God, the Full Gospel Business Men, where your life will bloom like the rose that you are.

Richard had worked alongside his father in the early years. From the second convention of the Fellowship, where he was the youth leader, God began to show him what he should do in the meetings, who to ask to participate, much in the same way as God had shown Demos. In the years leading up to his father's death and subsequently, many prophetic words had been given indicating that Richard should succeed in leading the Fellowship.

At a men's camp in Redlands, California, back in 1987, when Richard was not in leadership, the speaker suddenly turned, pointing to Richard, who was sitting a long way from him at the end of the platform. He said he had a word from God to the effect that Richard would follow in the steps of his father and would move in leadership, because God had ordained him. He was told not to be afraid; God would give Richard the blessings of Abraham, Isaac and Jacob; that he would be unmoveable if he fastened his eyes upon Jehovah-Jireh.

Another word of the Lord came through Ulf Ekman: 'You know your calling, you are called to carry that which your father was given from heaven.' Later in the prophecy he spoke of the crowds that Richard would see, something God has brought to pass in Armenia and, during 1999, in Central America.

A few years after these prophecies, when Richard and Vangie went to Moscow to sit under the ministry of Ulf Ekman, the Lord again spoke through him, telling Richard to be bold and courageous. God also said that there was a mantle, a mandate, a calling and an anointing for a new time, new ways, new peoples, new waves. Richard would lead with strength and easiness because he had an anointing to lead. In the same meeting, God spoke to Vangie concerning the close union between her and Richard and how God had heard her interceding on her husband's behalf. The Lord said she, too, was anointed and would receive greater wisdom.

There is no doubt that God has anointed Richard in his calling. New things have been happening in the Fellowship over the last two or three years. The wonderful outpouring in Hungary and, more recently, in Central America came as a result of visions God gave him. Time and again the Lord has spoken, to the effect that, although wonderful things have taken place in and through the FGBMFI in the past, they are nothing to what is going to happen in the future. The 'awakening giant', that army of laymen, is on its feet and beginning to move!

Appendix C

Ladies of the Fellowship

Over the last few years, the role of wives in the Fellowship has come very much into focus. While it is acknowledged that the main thrust is to reach out to men, it is appreciated that men could not give themselves to the work of the FGBMFI without the support of their wives. Increasingly, also, the need for ladies to be able to testify and minister to others has been recognized, and opportunity is being given through this integral organization.

Vangie Shakarian felt that God was calling her to organize the ladies in a new way and to give them an opportunity of being recognized. Ladies of the Fellowship gives those wives and ladies who support the FGBMFI official membership, with a pin to wear and a booklet outlining the many ways in which they can support their husbands and the local chapter. To this end, prayer meetings as well as days or weekends of teaching provide a means of ladies developing their ministry within the Fellowship.

Setting up this new group is not an indication that wives have played little part in the past. On the contrary, in the very beginning it was Rose who gave Demos the prophecy while he was receiving the vision from God. She travelled widely with her husband, and spoke at many conventions and meetings. Ladies of the Fellowship is an official recognition of the work continuing to be done by the ladies.

In one of the American *Voice* magazines, a report is given entitled 'A Full Gospel Business Men's Accolade'. This acknowledges the invaluable work done by the women by highlighting one lady from Alabama. For six years she prayed for the formation of a chapter in her city, and eventually called together about a dozen Spirit-filled men to her home. God honoured her prayers as a chapter was set up, and she took on the responsibility of writing and mailing the monthly newsletter and all announcements for the chapter, in addition to handling telephone calls and correspondence. Each year she would hold a dinner party for all FGBMFI members and wives, which she personally prepared for 75 to 100 people. Every year she would offer herself to work in the world convention as well as regional and state conventions. This continued until the lady was well into her seventies.

In most conventions around the world, ladies' meetings are held which they organize and run, arranging speakers, giving testimonies and ministering. At a local chapter level, many now have regular ladies' prayer meetings to support the work of the Fellowship, as well as ladies' evenings and teaching days or weekends. These give opportunity to train ladies in leading people to accept Jesus as Saviour and praying for the baptism in the Holy Spirit, and also encourage them to minister alongside their husbands.

Appendix D

Quotes from Writers

Rev. E. Davies, *I Will Pour Out My Spirit* (p. 205)

The 1960s saw the development of the Charismatic Movement in the mainline denominations, following the birth in the 1950s of the Full Gospel Business Men's Fellowship International under the leadership of Demos Shakarian, a friend and disciple of Charles Price and Oral Roberts, two Pentecostal healing evangelists. The movement spread rapidly among Episcopalians, Lutherans, Roman Catholics, and eventually among all denominations and throughout the world ... It has undoubtedly brought spiritual life and awareness to millions.

Dr Vinson Synan (FGBMFI Operations Chapter Manual)

Full Gospel Business Men's Fellowship International (FGBMFI) is perhaps the largest and most important Christian laymen's organization ... in the world ... The openness of the Fellowship to the Charismatic renewal in the mainline churches after 1960 created a historic role for FGBMFI as the chapters and conventions became major platforms for early leaders from all the churches including the Roman Catholics. Furthermore, FGBMFI's *Voice* became the major publication of record for several years to those whose testimonies fuelled the renewal both in America, and in other nations.

Without them, it is doubtful if the Charismatic movement would have developed as broadly as it did, or as fast as it did. In fact, in 1945 all the Pentecostals or Charismatic Christians in the world numbered only 16 million persons. By 1992, that figure had ballooned to 411 million people making up about 25 per cent of all the Christians in the world. A large part of that growth could be credited to the efforts of Full Gospel Business Men's Fellowship International.

Stanley M. Burgess and Gary B. McGee, eds, *Dictionary of Pentecostal and Charismatic Movements*

The original vision of the FGBMFI was of a non-sectarian fellowship of laity who could come together to share what God had done in their lives without any apology – even if that testimony included healing or tongues or deliverance from demonic forces. The impact of the FGBMFI on the Pentecostal and Charismatic movements has been considerable and not without controversy. The typical meeting usually held in a hotel ballroom or a restaurant was often a marked departure from the Pentecostal meeting of the past. The FGBMFI took the message of the power of the gospel to heal and deliver and of the baptism of the Holy Spirit from the tents to the hotels and convention centres of America. Often speakers were laymen who told of God's remarkable and miraculous intervention in their lives and businesses. They offered prayer for the sick and many were saved, healed and filled with the Holy Spirit in these services. This was certainly not the traditional revivalist meeting of the past, nor was it like any of the usual interdenominational testimony meetings. Many of the traditional ministers from Pentecostal denominations could not adjust to this new approach; and although the stress was that the FGBMFI was not a replacement for the local church, many pastors felt threatened by this open ecumenical fellowship.

'Demos Shakarian Receives Award for Charismatic Leadership', *Voice* magazine, 1987

Ten thousand Christian leaders were present in New Orleans, Louisiana as Demos Shakarian received an award for his leadership in the Charismatic renewal. Also honoured were David Du Plessis and Oral Roberts. The award, given by the North American Congress on the Holy Spirit and World Evangelization, states in part, 'For his prophetic leadership in founding and leading the Full Gospel Business Men's Fellowship International thereby raising up a worldwide army of Spirit-filled lay witnesses to Jesus Christ, we, the leaders and participants in the North American Congress on the Holy Spirit and World Evangelization, do present this award.'

The award is signed by Vinson Synan, Chairman of the North American Renewal Service Committee, and indicates Demos' life-long dedication to the building up of a body of lay people in these last days that will take the Gospel of Jesus Christ into the business and secular community.

John and Elizabeth Sherrill, Foreword to *Catching the Vision* by Val Fotherby

On our most recent visit to the United Kingdom ... we visited a dozen chapters of the Full Gospel Business Men's Fellowship over a period of four months. On each occasion we came away impressed ... Impressed by the continual emphasis on the church (the local churches of varying denominations) as the body of Christ, and the Fellowship as a service to, never a substitute for, that church.

D.W. Bebbington, *Evangelicalism in Modern Britain* (p. 231)

The Full Gospel Business Men's Fellowship International, an American body founded by a Pentecostal layman to organize Christian dinner gatherings, fostered the spread of spiritual gifts by holding a much publicized convention in London in 1965 and by establishing chapters in many parts of the country subsequently.

A.C. Valdez, Sr, with James F. Scheer, *Fire on Azusa Street* (p. 113)

Demos Shakarian managed some of my meetings, two of which made evangelical history: a colossal tent meeting at Whittier and Goodrich in East Los Angeles, and another in Fresno (three weeks of ministering) where hundreds received Christ.

I am grateful to Demos – not only for what he did then, but for what he has done since then: guiding and stimulating growth of the Full Gospel Business Men's Fellowship International which, through chapters all over the world, has brought countless millions to Christ. My gratitude goes also to Demos' lovely and gracious wife Rose, who has always been a source of spiritual blessing and strength to him.

It is my strong conviction that the Full Gospel Business Men's Fellowship International is playing a tremendous part in the worldwide charismatic breakthrough, a greater spiritual breakthrough than that of Martin Luther's day, for this one will end in the return of Jesus Christ.

Rev. John Stride, Appendix to *Catching the Vision* by Val Fotherby

I can commend it (FGBMFI) as a fellowship that God is using in our time and in our land. At the heart of the FGBMFI's philosophy is the role of personal testimony. My personal testimony is that for myself, my wife and upwards of a dozen of my parishioners, the local chapter of the Full Gospel Business Men's Fellowship International has been a source of encouragement, challenge and spiritual growth. We have all at last seen God at work. And some of us can never be the same again, because God has used FGBMFI dinners when he has filled us with his Holy Spirit or made us whole or given us a new power to live the Christian life.

I am grateful for that first invitation to a chapter dinner and glad that I didn't wait until I could dot every 'i' and cross every 't' with the FGBMFI before going along and discovering that God can use the vision of a Californian Armenian dairy farmer to bless and to build His church in England.

Notes

Chapter 1

1 FGBMFI Operation Manual, p. 7.

Chapter 2

1 See Appendix A for more details of the prophecy.
2 Vinson Synan, *Under His Banner*, p. 60.
3 Tommy Ashcraft, *Prodigal Husband*, p. 127.
4 *ibid.*, p. 131.

Chapter 3

1 Stanley M. Burgess and Gary B. McGee, eds, *Dictionary of Pentecostal and Charismatic Movements*, p. 321.
2 Orval Brooks, 'Sound the Alarm', *Voice* magazine (USA), volume 25, no. 10.
3 Bill Phipps, with Dorothy Tuttle, *The Final Hours*, pp. 18–23.
4 John Steitz, 'Broken Barriers', *Voice* magazine (USA), volume 26, no. 5.
5 Demos Shakarian, *Voice* magazine (USA), volume 40, no. 4.

6 Demos Shakarian, *Voice* magazine (USA).
7 John and Elizabeth Sherrill, *The Happiest People on Earth*, pp. 188–91.

Chapter 4

1 Vinson Synan, *Under His Banner*, p. 74.
2 Ray Barnett was later to head Friends in the West, a human rights organization that aimed to help Christians behind the then Iron Curtain, which took him all over Europe and Africa and eventually into the Lebanon, where they were able to bring much needed aid to that war-torn country. His story is told in the book by Leila Gilbert, *Where the Brave Dare Not Go*.
3 Val Fotherby, *Catching the Vision*, p. 23.

Chapter 5

1 *From the Kwai to the Kingdom*, quoted in Val Fotherby, *Catching the Vision*, p. 24.

Chapter 6

1 A report to the Home Office by the Board of Visitors to the Wolds Remand Prison.

Chapter 7

1 *Airlift to London*.
2 Vinson Synan, *Under His Banner*, p. 78.

Chapter 9

1 Ulrich and Barbara von Schnurbein, 'A Different Goal', *Voice* magazine (Europe), no. 921.
2 This short article, entitled 'Looking Back – First Airlift to France from the USA', was written by Fred and Joyce

Doerflein in 1987, and recently republished in *Global Outreach News*, airlift information put out by the Seattle Chapter.

3 'To France, with Love', *Voice* magazine (USA), volume 26, no. 7.

4 The last chapter of *The Happiest People on Earth* is entitled 'The Golden Chain', which describes how Demos saw the work of the FGBMFI.

5 Lynn Heritage, UK Editor, *Voice* magazine, *Networking* no. 9902, 2 April 1999.

6 Sherrill, *The Happiest People on Earth*.

7 *Networking* no. 981, 1 January 1998.

8 *Networking* no. 971, 4 April 1997.

Chapter 10

1 Part of the report given by Dario, *Voice* magazine (USA) volume 41, no. 3.

2 *Voice* magazine (USA), volume 27, no. 1.

3 See Chapter 15 for the story.

4 *Voice* magazine (USA) volume 41, no. 11.

Chapter 12

1 Allan Jones' personal report of his visit to the southern hemisphere, 1992.

2 *Australian Voice* magazine no. 6.

3 *ibid.*

4 *Australian Voice* magazine.

5 *South Pacific Voice* magazine no. 1.

Chapter 14

1 Jimmy Hughes, 'The Godfollower', *Voice* magazine (USA) volume 47, no. 3.

2 Rudy Rivera, 'The Source', *Voice* magazine (Europe) no. 986.

3 *ibid.*

4   Sir Lionel A. Luckhoo, 'The Lion of Guyana', *Voice* magazine
    (USA) volume 42, no. 7.
5   *ibid*.
6   *ibid*.

Bibliography

Airlift to London, Full Gospel Business Men's Fellowship International, Costa Mesa 1966.

Archer, Fred, *Sir Lionel*, Gift Publications, Costa Mesa 1980.

Ashcraft, Tommy, with Call, Max, *Prodigal Husband*, Gift Publications, Costa Mesa 1980.

Burgess, Stanley M. and McGee, Gary B., *Dictionary of Pentecostal and Charismatic Movements*, Zondervan, Michigan 1993.

Davies, R.E., *I Will Pour Out My Spirit*, Monarch, Tunbridge Wells 1992.

Fotherby, Valerie, *Catching the Vision*, Kingsway, Eastbourne 1989.

Gilbert, Leila, *Where The Brave Dare Not Go*, Life Journey Books, Illinois 1987.

Johnson, James E., with Balsiger, David W., *Beyond Defeat*, private publication 1978.

Lightle, Steve, *Operation Exodus II*, Insight Publishing, Tulsa 1998.

Lightle, Steve, with Muhlan, Eberhard and Fortune, Katie, *Exodus II*, Hunter Books, Kingwood 1983.

Phipps, Bill, with Tuttle, Dorothy, *The Final Hours*, Picorp, Minsk 1993.

Price, Dr Charles S., *The Real Faith*, Logos International, New Jersey 1972.

Shakarian, Demos, *The Ultimate Dimension*, Full Gospel Business Men's Fellowship International, Costa Mesa (no date).

Shakarian, Demos, *The Vision Intensified*, Full Gospel Business Men's Fellowship International, Costa Mesa (no date).

Shakarian, Demos, *Behold the Glory of God*, Full Gospel Business Men's Fellowship International, Costa Mesa 1988.

Shakarian, Demos, *Divine Life*, Full Gospel Business Men's Fellowship International, Costa Mesa 1991.

Sherrill, John and Elizabeth, *The Happiest People on Earth*, Hodder & Stoughton, London 1996.

Sherry, Norman, B. *Discover Your Miracles*, Pinecrest Publications, New York 1996.

Synan, Vinson, *Under His Banner*, Gift Publications, Costa Mesa 1992.

Valdez, A.C., Sr, with Scheer, James F., *Fire on Azusa Street*, Gift Publications, Costa Mesa 1980.

Whittaker, Colin, *Great Revivals*, Marshall, Morgan & Scott, Basingstoke 1984.

In addition, many issues of *Voice* magazine and the Internet publication *Networking* at www.fgbmfi.org.

Audio Tapes

Shakarian, Demos, Hicks, Tommy and Shakarian, Richard, *FGBMFI Historical Highlights*.

Shakarian, Richard, *Great Generals of the Cross*.

Shakarian, Richard, *School of Success*.

Video Tapes

Demos Shakarian and others, *The Turning Point*, a compilation of testimonies from various conventions.

Audio and video tapes can be obtained from:

Full Gospel Business Men's Fellowship International
20 Corporate Park Drive
3rd Floor
Irvine
California
CA 92606-5116

tel: 00 1 949 260 0700
fax: 00 1 949 260 0718
website: http://www.fgbmfi.org
e-mail: fgbmfi@Ix.netcom.com

UK *Voice* magazines can be obtained from:

FGBMFI Office
PO Box 11
Knutsford
Cheshire
WA16 6QP

tel: 01565 632667
fax: 01565 755639

Also available from HarperCollins*Publishers*:

The Final Frontier

Incredible Stories of Near-Death Experiences

Richard Kent and Val Fotherby

Where do we go when we die? And is there really such a place as hell?

Here are more than twenty stories from people who are convinced of the existence of the afterlife – because they've been there. Their near-death experiences followed anything from heart attacks to car crashes, and every person who tells their amazing story is convinced that they have seen what is beyond the final frontier of death.

Some tell of wonderful experiences of heaven and the happiness they felt there. Others recall the spine-chilling moments when they realized that they were in a place they are convinced was hell …

Christian Books

Timeless truths in shifting times

www.christian-publishing.com

News from a Christian perspective

Exclusive author interviews

Read extracts from the latest books

Share thoughts and faith

Complete list of signing events

Full catalogue & ordering

www.christian-publishing.com